THE
KNITTER'S
HANDBOOK

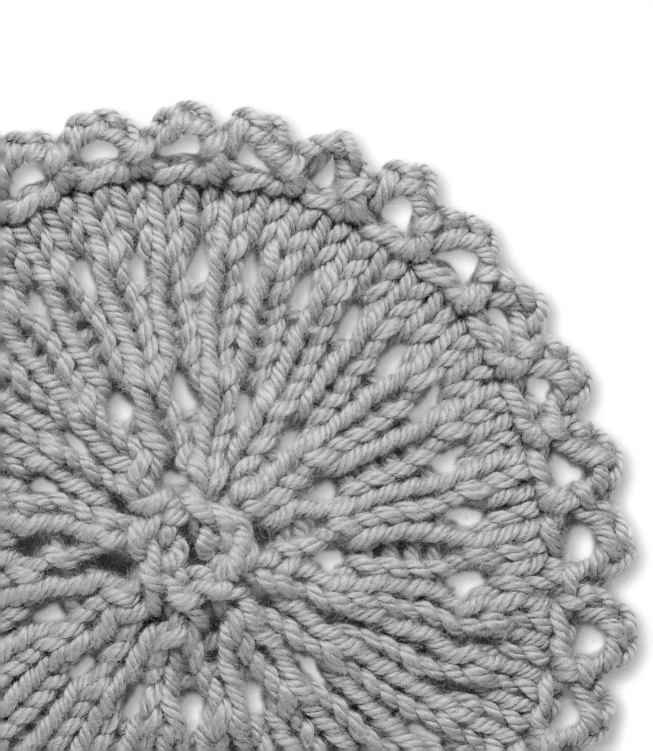

Eleanor Van Zandt

THE KNITTER'S HANDBOOK

Yarns • Needles • Stitches • Techniques

hamlyn

An Hachette UK Company
www.hachette.co.uk

First published in Great Britain in 2006 by Hamlyn,
a division of Octopus Publishing Group Ltd
Endeavour House, 189 Shaftesbury Avenue
London WC2H 8JY
www.octopusbooks.co.uk
www.octopusbooksusa.com

First published in paperback in 2009

Distributed in the U.S. and Canada by Octopus
Books USA:
c/o Hachette Book Group
237 Park Avenue
New York NY 10017

ISBN: 978-0-600-61941-3

A CIP catalogue record for this book is available from
the British Library

Printed and bound in China

10 9 8 7 6 5 4

Note
Some of the material in this book has previously
appeared in *The Hamlyn Complete Knitting Course.*

contents

abbreviations

beg beginning

ch chain

cm centimetre(s)

cont continu(e)(ing)

C2[4:6]B cable 2[4:6] back (see page 102)

C2[4:6]F cable 2[4:6] forward (see page 102)

Cr2B cross 2 back (see page 103)

Cr2F cross 2 front (see page 103)

dc double crochet

dec decrease(e)(ing)

foll follow(ing)

g st garter stitch (knit every row)

inc increas(e)(ing)

K knit

kw knitwise

LH left hand

M1 make 1: pick up strand between stitch just worked and next stitch on LH needle and knit into back of it

mm millimetre(s)

oz ounce(s)

P purl

patt pattern

psso pass slipped stitch over

pw purlwise

rem remain(ing)

rep repeat

rev st st reverse stocking/stockinette stitch (1 row P, 1 row K)

RH right hand

RS right side

skpo slip1, knit 1, pass slipped stitch over

sl slip

sl st slip stitch/crochet

st(s) stitch(es)

st st stocking/stockinette stitch (1 row K, 1 row P)

tbl through back of loop(s)

tog together

Tw2PL Twist 2 left purlwise (see page 100)

Tw2PR Twist 2 right purlwise (see page 100)

Tw2L Twist 2 left (see page 99)

Tw2R Twist 2 right (see page 99)

WS wrong side

wyb with yarn at back

wyf with yarn at front

yf yarn forward

yon yarn over needle

yrn yarn round needle

introduction

In recent years there has been a revival of interest in knitting. Top designers have demonstrated that this versatile craft is capable of producing high-fashion garments. Yarn manufacturers vie with each other in producing yarns designed for a wide spectrum of knit-wear – from classic designs, traditionally knitted in high-quality wool, to practical, easy-care garments for children to glamorous, extravagant fashions for evening. In short, the creative possibilities of knitting have never been greater.

This book will introduce you to the pleasures of knitting and help you to develop the techniques you need to tackle any knitting pattern. 'The basics' provides information on yarns and the simple, inexpensive equipment required and describes the basic knitting skills: the knit stitch, the purl stitch, casting on and casting/binding off.

'Knitting a project' shows you how to follow a knitting pattern and construct a garment. Once you have grasped the simple but crucial principle of achieving the right tension/gauge and can shape a fabric and pick up stitches, you can consider yourself a capable knitter.

The following three sections will greatly enlarge your repertoire of techniques, enabling you to produce appealing textured fabrics including cables, bobbles and smocking; tubular fabric and medallions and the whole variety of multicoloured effects.

'Embellishments' demonstrates how you can use decorative techniques and trimmings to give a plain knitted garment a distinctive finishing touch. This is followed by a section containing a variety of sophisticated techniques – such as invisible casting/binding on and off, grafting and working a hem – which will increase your expertise and give your work a professional finish.

All of the sections include a collection of stitch patterns appropriate to the topics covered in them, and throughout the book you will find hints for making your knitting easier and more successful.

the basics

The act of transforming a ball of yarn into a beautifully knitted garment may seem daunting – if you've never done it before. But knitting is actually easy.

This section provides information on yarn types and the simple, inexpensive equipment required for knitting. It shows you how to master the knit and purl stitches, and how to cast on and cast/bind off. These basic knitting techniques will be the foundation of all your future projects.

yarns

Much of the pleasure of knitting lies in the yarn itself. Hand knitting is a very tactile activity, and a yarn that is pleasing to touch and appropriate for the project will add enormously to both your enjoyment of the work and your pride in the finished garment.

There is a vast range of yarns available today – not only the classic smooth yarns, which never go out of fashion, but also a dazzling variety of unusual textures and fibres, from glossy silk, to velvety chenille, to chunky bouclé. The endless creative possibilities they offer are one good reason for learning to design your own knitting; but even if you are using a published pattern, as most knitters do, you will find it worthwhile to become familiar with the different yarns available so that you can make a wise choice of yarn and pattern.

fibre content

Yarns are made of many different fibres and combinations of fibres, both natural and synthetic.

natural fibres

Wool is the traditional favourite among natural fibres. It is warm, relatively lightweight and elastic. This last quality makes it easy to knit with and means that the finished garment will – if cared for properly – hold its shape. Some wools are even machine washable.

Wool varies considerably in texture, according to the sheep from which it came and the spinning and finishing methods applied to it. The softest quality is Botany wool, which comes from merino sheep raised in Australia. Lambswool, too, is very soft, coming from the first shearing of the young animal.

Mohair is the fluffy hair of the angora goat. Despite its delicate appearance, it is strong, though not very elastic. Kid mohair is softer than ordinary mohair from the adult animal, and more expensive. Mohair is often combined with other fibres, such as wool or acrylic, for economy.

Angora is the fur of the angora rabbit. It is feather-soft and very expensive. Because it has a tendency to shed, it is not recommended for garments for babies, who might choke on the fibres.

Cashmere comes from the Himalayan goat. An extremely soft and luxurious fibre, it is usually blended with other fibres.

Alpaca is the hair of the llama. It is often added to wool yarns to provide extra softness.

Silk, which is spun from the cocoon of the silkworm, is a luxurious fibre with a strength that belies its softness. Pure silk yarn normally has a glossy finish and comes in beautifully rich colours. Silk is also found combined with other fibres, such as wool and mohair.

Cotton is obtained from the seed heads of the cotton plant. Yarns made of cotton are

This assortment of yarns gives an idea of the marvellous variety of textures available.

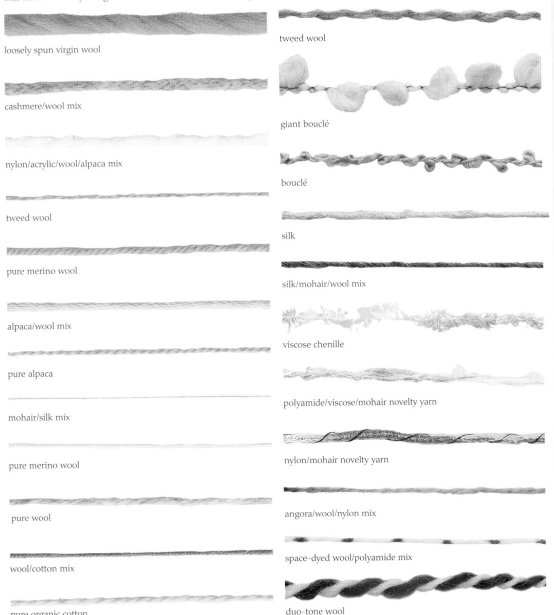

loosely spun virgin wool

cashmere/wool mix

nylon/acrylic/wool/alpaca mix

tweed wool

pure merino wool

alpaca/wool mix

pure alpaca

mohair/silk mix

pure merino wool

pure wool

wool/cotton mix

pure organic cotton

tweed wool

giant bouclé

bouclé

silk

silk/mohair/wool mix

viscose chenille

polyamide/viscose/mohair novelty yarn

nylon/mohair novelty yarn

angora/wool/nylon mix

space-dyed wool/polyamide mix

duo-tone wool

cool and so are ideal for summer garments. Although it can be somewhat expensive, cotton is generally hard-wearing and good value. Cotton that has been mercerized is particularly strong and lustrous. Cotton's only drawbacks are its lack of elasticity, which makes it rather difficult to knit with, and its density, which makes it slow to dry after laundering.

Linen is a very strong fibre, taken from the stem of the flax plant. It has a naturally slubbed texture and is often combined with cotton.

synthetic fibres

Synthetic fibres have certain practical advantages over most natural fibres, being strong, lightweight, resistant to moths and, in many cases, machine washable. For these reasons, they are often added to natural fibres.

The main synthetic fibres are **acrylic**, **polyamide**, (including nylon), **polyester**, and **viscose** (including rayon). Of these, the commonest is acrylic, which is very soft and lightweight. Acrylics are often used to achieve novel textures and characteristics that are not available with natural fibres. A special category of synthetic is the **metallic fibres**, which are derived from aluminium.

Yarns made of 100 percent synthetic fibres are not so satisfying to use as those made of natural fibres or natural-synthetic blends. They are less pleasing to the touch, and garments made from them have a tendency to lose their shape.

construction

The character of a yarn is determined not only by its fibre content, but also by the spinning and finishing methods used in its manufacture.

size

Yarns vary enormously in size, or thickness (also called their weight). The smooth, so-called 'classic' yarns fall into seven categories: two-ply, three-ply, four-ply, double knitting, Aran-weight, chunky and extra-chunky. Within these categories there is some variation, but it is usually possible to substitute one yarn for another in the same category.

The word 'ply' is used in two ways. Literally, it means an individual strand of fibre. A ply can be of any thickness; therefore, a yarn consisting of two plies might well be thicker than one containing four. However, in categorizing yarns we use the names 'two-ply', 'three-ply' and 'four-ply' to designate yarns that not only are so constructed but also conform to an accepted size category. Moreover, a textured yarn may also be described in relation to these categories; for example, 'knits as four-ply' means that the yarn (irrespective of its construction) will yield roughly the same number of stitches and rows over a given measurement as a standard four-ply yarn. This information is especially useful if you are substituting a yarn or designing a garment from scratch.

finish

In the spinning process, there is a range of different finishes which may be applied to the fibres. The plies may be twisted loosely or firmly, to produce a wide range of textures, from soft to very firm. In general, the tighter the twist, the harder-wearing the yarn.

Slubbed yarns are irregularly spun, so that they have thick and thin stretches.

They give a pleasing variation of texture to plain stitch patterns, but are less successful than the smooth yarns when worked in complex stitch patterns, as they tend to obscure the detail somewhat; however, they can be quite effective in some larger lace and cable patterns.

Bouclé yarns have a crinkly texture produced by catching up one of the plies so that it forms a little loop around the other(s).

Knop yarns are similar in construction to bouclé yarns, but more irregular, with large loops at more widely spaced intervals. They produce a fuzzy, knobbly fabric.

Chenille yarns have a dense, velvety texture. Although very attractive, they are not easy to knit with.

Multicoloured effects can be produced by spinning together plies of different colours, or, for a subtler effect, different shades of the same colour. Flecked tweed yarns are the classic example of a multicoloured yarn. From time to time, fashion favours the technique of space-dyeing yarns, so that the colours change along the length. Such yarns can be fun to use, although you may sometimes find that you prefer the effect in the ball to that of the knitted fabric.

Novelty yarns appear and disappear along with the latest fashion trends. They may include woven ribbon and rag yarns, blends of metallic and cotton fibres, thin strands of suede – whatever is currently in vogue.

The choice of yarns available at a given time is, of course, dictated by the current fashion. When the fashion is for colour-patterned knitting, the more unusual textures, which do not lend themselves to these designs, tend to disappear.

buying yarn

When buying yarn, it is important to read the information on the ball band. This will include the fibre content, blocking/pressing instructions, recommendations for care of the garment, and the weight of the ball or skein. In some cases it may also give a recommended needle size and the number of stitches and rows produced in stocking (stockinette) stitch using those needles (see 'Tension/Gauge', page 50). This last information is very useful if you wish to substitute a different yarn for the one recommended by the pattern.

One essential piece of information on the ball band is the dye lot number. Make sure that all the yarn is from the same dye lot, for even a minor variation can be quite noticeable on the garment. Buy all the yarn required for the garment at the same time; later on, that particular dye lot may no longer be available.

If you are not fortunate enough to live near a good yarn shop, don't despair. Some shops offer a mail-order service, and there are many mail-order suppliers.

The five basic weights of smooth yarn.

4-ply (100% alpaca)

double knitting (dk) (100% cotton)

Aran (55% merino, 33% microfibre, 12% cashmere)

chunky (100% alpaca)

super chunky (50% wool, 50% alpaca)

This yarn label (right) gives all the information a purchaser might need, including the recommended needles and suggested tension/gauge over stocking/ stockinette stitch.

Warm (40°C) Wool Cycle, minimum machine action

Warm iron
160°C

Do not bleach

A Dry cleanable
in all solvents

Do not tumble dry
Dry flat out of direct sunlight

50 g
Approx Length 183 m (200 yds)

10 cm

10 cm   36 rows

28 sts

10   3¼
UK   mm
3
US

100% MERINO WOOL
4PLY

equipment

Little in the way of special equipment is required for hand knitting. The one essential item, of course, is the needles. These come in a variety of sizes (see page 252) and types, which you can acquire gradually as the need arises. There are also various other accessories that will come in handy occasionally; their uses are described on pages 16–17.

Needles are made of several different materials: metal and plastic are the commonest today, but bamboo and sometimes wood can also be found. Metal needles are generally the easiest to work with, as the stitches slide easily along them; plastic tends to be rather sticky, although some people prefer it because it is warmer to the touch. You may sometimes find needles with rigid points that are attached to a flexible length of plastic. These are useful for knitting heavy items, as the whole weight of the work does not need to be supported by the hands.

Other types of needle include circular and double-pointed needles, for working in the round, and cable needles, used in cable stitch patterns.

If you take good care of your needles they should last for many years. Store them in a large flat box or special needle case, so that they do not become bent. Never use a needle with a jagged point, as it can catch in and split the yarn.

Equipment needed for knitting. Some of these items are essential, some optional.

Plastic needles
Metal needles
Bamboo needles

Crochet hook – used for working crocheted edges and button loops and for darning in yarn ends

Set of four double-pointed needles – used for tubular knitting and for medallions

Cable needle – the bend prevents the held stitches from slipping off; a straight cable needle will do the job

Circular needle (also called a twin pin) – used for tubular or straight knitting

Tape measure

Ring markers – used to mark the beginning of rounds in tubular knitting and certain key points in a pattern

Stitch stoppers or needle guards – used to prevent the work from slipping off the needle when it is put away; an elastic band will serve the same purpose, but stoppers will also protect the needle points

Knitter's pins – used for holding two sections together when seaming and for marking divisions on edges when picking up a specified number of stitches

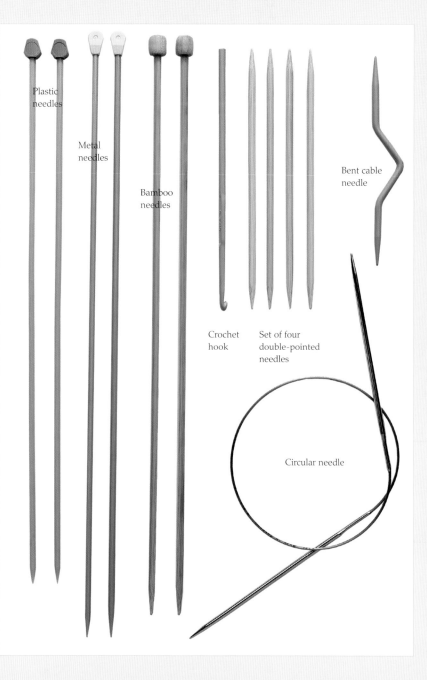

Plastic needles

Metal needles

Bamboo needles

Bent cable needle

Crochet hook

Set of four double-pointed needles

Circular needle

Glass-headed pins – used for blocking pieces of knitting

Tapestry needle – used for seaming and for working embroidery on knitting

Row counter

Bobbin – used for holding small amounts of yarn when working with two or more colours across a row

Safety pins

Stitch holder – a double-pointed needle or a length of yarn may be used instead; ordinary safety pins are best where only a few stitches need to be held

Needle gauge – useful for checking sizes of double-pointed and circular needles (marked only on the package) and when using needles sized according to a different system from the one used in the pattern

Other useful equipment includes scissors for cutting yarn (a pair of embroidery scissors is also useful, especially when undoing work knitted with fuzzy yarns), a spray bottle for wet blocking, an iron, a cotton pressing cloth and an ironing board with a well-padded surface. A purpose-made knitting bag is a handy way of keeping your knitting clean and tidy; some bags have wooden frames which allow them to stand on the floor when in use and then fold up for carrying or storing. A folder or notebook for storing patterns is also useful.

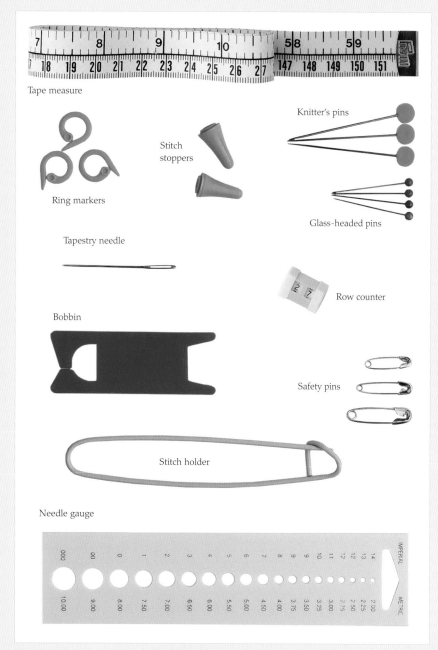

Tape measure

Ring markers

Stitch stoppers

Knitter's pins

Glass-headed pins

Tapestry needle

Row counter

Bobbin

Safety pins

Stitch holder

Needle gauge

casting on

The first step in beginning a piece of knitting is to place the required number of stitches on the needle. This is called casting on. There are several different methods of casting on. The most commonly used cast-on methods are the thumb method and the cable method. Both of these require the yarn to be held as for knitting, so turn to pages 22–23 to see which way of holding the yarn you prefer. The single cast-on is the simplest method; however, because the loops formed are difficult to work into evenly, it is not recommended for the novice. The double cast-on may look like a form of cat's cradle, but it does have the benefit of needing no knitting experience.

slip knot
For the single cast-on, thumb and cable methods, begin by making a slip knot on the needle. First make a loop in the yarn. Slip the point of the needle through the loop, then pull on both ends of the yarn to tighten the knot.

single cast-on
This method produces a soft, flexible edge. Begin by making a slip knot near the end of the yarn. Wind the yarn around the thumb, and hold it with three fingers.

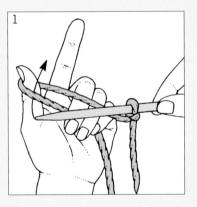

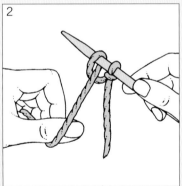

1 Bring the needle up through the loop as shown by the arrow.

2 Slip the thumb out of the loop, and use it to pull the yarn gently downwards, forming a stitch. Repeat steps 1 and 2.

cable method

This method produces an attractive, smooth edge, suitable for various fabrics. Begin with a slip knot near the end of the yarn.

1 Holding the loose end firmly, insert the right-hand (RH) needle under the left, to the left of the slip knot. Take the main yarn under and over the (RH) needle, from left to right.

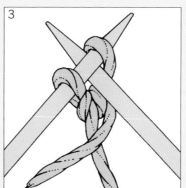

2 Draw the loop on the (RH) needle through to the front, and place it over the left-hand (LH) needle.

3 Insert the (RH) needle between the two stitches. Take the yarn under and over it, as in step 2, draw the loop through, and place it on the needle. Repeat steps 1–3.

thumb method

The edge produced by this method is the same as for the double cast-on. Multiply the number of stitches by 2 cm (¾ in) and measure off this length of yarn; make a slip knot slightly beyond this point. Hold the short end of yarn in your left hand as shown. Wrap the yarn from the ball around the little finger of your right hand, as for knitting (see page 22).

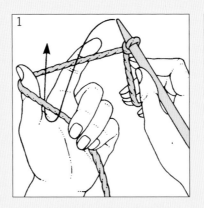

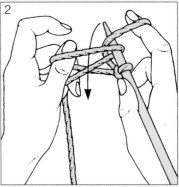

1 Take the point of the needle up under the front strand of yarn lying between the fingers and thumb of the left hand, following the direction of the arrow.

2 Now bring the right-hand (ball) yarn under and over the point of the needle. Holding both lengths fairly taut, bring the needle down through the left-hand loop as shown by the arrow.

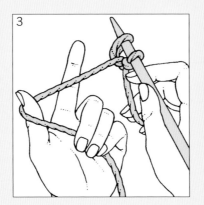

3 Slip the thumb out of the loop, and use it to pull on the short end of yarn as shown to complete the new stitch. Repeat steps 1–3.

tip

If you tend to cast on tightly, use needles a size or two larger than specified by the pattern for the casting on. Then change to the correct needles for the first row.

double cast-on

Multiply the number of stitches required by 2 cm (¾ in), and measure off this length of yarn. Wind the yarn around the fingers of your left hand as shown: up between the third and little fingers, around the little finger, over all four fingers, then clockwise around the thumb; finally take the yarn between the second and third fingers and hold it gently but firmly. Spread the thumb and index finger apart to tension the yarn.

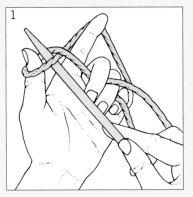

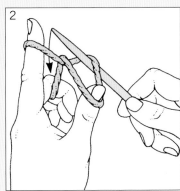

1 Slip the point of the needle up through the thumb loop.

2 Take it over and under the yarn extending to the index finger, thus forming a loop on the needle; as you do so, rotate your left hand towards you (you may do this instinctively, as it feels natural).

tip

For an extra-flexible edge, use the double or thumb method and use two needles, held together, instead of one. When the stitches have been cast on, remove one of the needles. The large loops will be easy to work into.

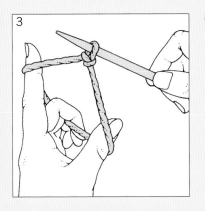

3 Bring the needle back through the thumb loop. Slip the thumb out of the loop and use it to pull down the free length of yarn. This completes the first stitch. Repeat steps 1–3. The edge produced is quite flexible, yet firm, and so is a good one for ribbing.

holding the yarn

Once you have cast some stitches onto a needle, you are ready to begin knitting. There are several ways of holding the yarn and needles; the two basic methods are shown here.

The right-hand method of holding the yarn is used mainly in English-speaking countries and the left-hand method is more commonly used in continental Europe. Each method produces exactly the same results. Try both and see which is more comfortable for you. It is a good idea to learn to use both methods, as some multicoloured knitting requires you to work with two different colours simultaneously.

Whichever method you use, the yarn must be wound loosely around the fingers to keep it slightly tensioned, so that the stitches will be smooth and even. You may find at first that you prefer to wrap the yarn twice around the little finger.

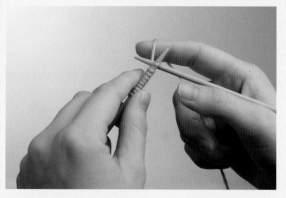
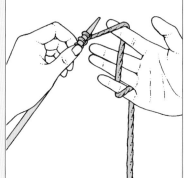

right-hand method

Take the needle with the cast-on stitches in the left hand. Wind the yarn around the fingers of the right hand as shown.

Take the needle in the right hand so that it lies between the thumb and the rest of the hand as shown (in practice, the needle is often picked up before the yarn). Insert the needle into the first stitch on the LH needle, and slide the right hand forward to take the yarn around the point of the RH needle. In the photograph the needles are shown forming the knit stitch.

tip

If you are left-handed, you may find the 'Continental' method of holding the yarn relatively easy to learn, as the work is more evenly divided between the two hands. The alternative is to use the right-hand method *reversed*, holding the needle with the stitches in the right hand, wrapping the yarn around the fingers of the left hand, and using the left hand to work the stitches. If you choose this method, you will find it helpful, when following the instructions in this book, to hold the book up to a mirror. (A mirror is not necessary if you use the left-hand method, as you can work exactly as shown.)

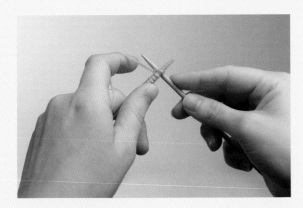

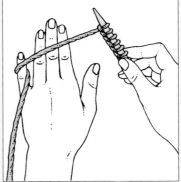

left-hand method

Take the needle with the cast-on stitches in the right hand. Wind the yarn around the fingers of the left hand as shown.

Transfer the needle with the stitches to the left hand, and raise the index finger to tension the yarn. Take the working needle in the right hand, with the thumb in front and the fingers in back. Insert the needle into the first stitch, then rotate the left hand to bring the yarn around the point of the needle. In the photograph the needles are shown forming the knit stitch.

knit and purl

Most knitting is based on combinations of just two basic stitches: the knit stitch and the purl stitch. Once you have mastered these two stitches, you can work many different stitch patterns.

Begin by casting on about 25 or 30 stitches, using a double-knitting yarn in a light colour, preferably all wool or a wool mix, for its resilience. Practise the knit stitch until you can work it fairly smoothly. Then practise the purl stitch.

Garter stitch (right). This simple stitch pattern is produced by knitting every row. The fabric has a distinct horizontal ridge and is quite stretchy.

the knit stitch

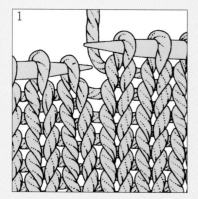

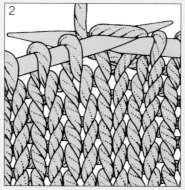

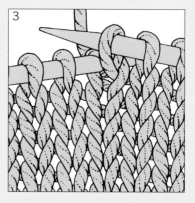

1 Hold the needle with the stitches to be knitted in the left hand with the yarn behind.

2 Insert the RH needle into a stitch from front to back. Take the yarn over it, forming a loop.

3 Bring the needle and the new loop to the front of the work, and slide the original stitch off the LH needle.

the purl stitch

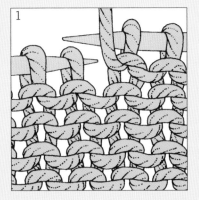 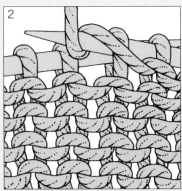 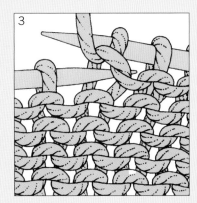

1 Hold the stitches to be purled in the left hand, with the yarn at the front of the work.

2 Insert the RH needle through the front of the stitch, from back to front. Take the yarn over and under, forming a loop.

3 Take the needle and the new loop through to the back; slide the stitch off the LH needle.

Stocking/stockinette stitch (right). The most widely used of all stitch patterns, this is produced by knitting all the stitches on the right-side rows and purling on the wrong-side rows. The fabric is very smooth and slightly elastic.

variations

Once you have learned to knit and purl, it is easy to learn a few variations on these basic techniques. One of these is working into the back of the stitch rather than into the front of it. This technique is sometimes required when increasing stitches (see pages 56–60) and in some stitch patterns.

It is possible to produce a variation of stocking/stockinette stitch by working all the knit stitches through the back; the purl stitches are worked through the front as usual. The fabric produced is unusually firm.

Another technique is simply to slip a stitch off the left-hand needle onto the right without working it. Slipped stitches are used in some methods of decreasing and in some multicolour patterns (see page 172).

knitting through the back of the loop

Insert the RH needle behind the LH needle and through the back of the stitch, and take the yarn under and over the needle, forming a knit stitch in the usual way. Pull the new stitch through, and slip the original stitch off the LH needle. The new stitch is slightly twisted.

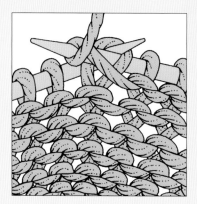

purling through the back of the loop

This involves turning the RH needle briefly to point from left to right, then inserting it from back to front through the back of the loop as shown. Form a purl stitch in the usual way, and slip the original stitch off the LH needle. The new stitch is slightly twisted.

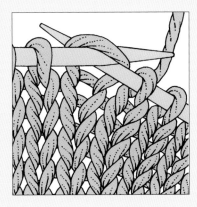

slipping a stitch knitwise

Insert the needle into the front of the stitch as if to knit it, but do not form a new stitch; simply slip the original stitch onto the RH needle. The same technique is used to slip a purl stitch knitwise.

Unless the pattern instructions state otherwise, the yarn is held as for the preceding stitch: at the back if this was a knit stitch; at the front if it was a purl stitch.

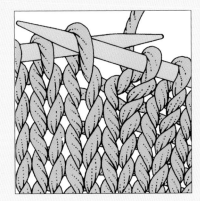

slipping a stitch purlwise

Insert the needle into the stitch from back to front, as if you were going to purl it, then simply slip it onto the RH needle. The same technique is used to slip a purl stitch purlwise.

Unless the pattern instructions state otherwise, the yarn is held as for the preceding stitch.

casting/binding off

To end a piece of knitting, you 'cast/bind off' the stitches. This technique is also used to reduce the number of stitches at the side of a piece of knitting – for example, when shaping an armhole – or in the middle, when working a horizontal buttonhole or, sometimes, when shaping a neckline. There are several methods of casting/binding off, but the most commonly used is the one shown here. This basic method is varied a little when casting/binding off a ribbed fabric; this produces a softer, slightly more elastic edge than the basic method.

It is very easy to make the mistake of casting/binding off too tightly, and producing an edge that is shorter than the width of the fabric. To avoid this, use a needle one or two sizes larger than those used for the main fabric when casting/binding off.

When you have learned the basic cast/bind-off method, try the advanced methods shown on pages 222–225.

basic cast/bind-off

1 Knit the first two stitches. Slip the LH needle into the first stitch on the RH needle.

2 Lift the first stitch over the second stitch and off the needle. Repeat steps 1 and 2 until one stitch remains. Break the yarn and draw it firmly through the last stitch.

If casting/binding off on the purled side of a stocking/stockinette stitch fabric, you may prefer to purl the stitches instead of knitting them. The loops of the cast/bound-off edge will thus lie toward the knit side of the work.

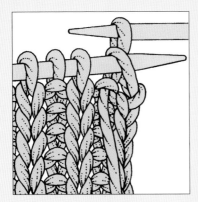

casting/binding off in rib

Work all the stitches as if continuing in the pattern: so purl stitches will be purled, rather than knitted. Lift the first stitch over the second as usual.

Achieving an even cast/bind-off in rib is not easy, even for experienced knitters. Practise on a spare piece of ribbing, keeping a fairly loose tension/gauge and working as evenly as possible.

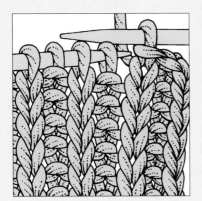

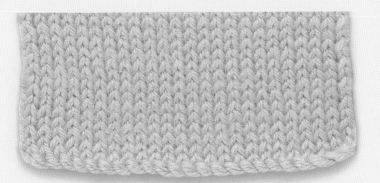

This stocking/stockinette stitch sample has been cast/bound off knitwise in the usual way.

simple textures

Some of the most popular stitch patterns are also among the simplest. These are combinations of knitting and purling. Cast on a number of stitches divisible by the stitch multiple, plus extra stitches as required.

moss/seed stitch

multiple of 2
Row 1 (RS) *K1, P1, rep from *.
Row 2 *P1, K1, rep from *.

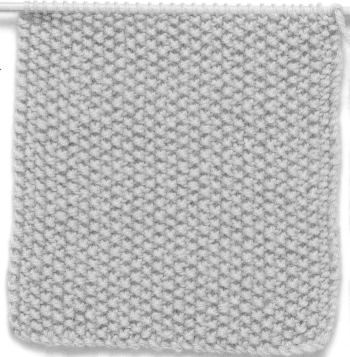

moss/seed stitch rib

multiple of 4 plus 3 extra
Row 1 (RS) *K3, P1, rep from * to last 3 sts, K3.
Row 2 K1, P1, K1, * K2, P1, K1, rep from *.

irish moss/seed stitch

multiple of 2
Rows 1 (RS) and 2 *K1, P1, rep
from *.
Rows 3 and 4 *P1, K1, rep from *.

diamond seed

multiple of 8
Row 1 (RS) *P1, K7, rep from *.
Rows 2 and 8 *K1, P5, K1, P1,
rep from *.
Rows 3 and 7 *K2, P1, K3, P1, K1,
rep from *.
Rows 4 and 6 *P2, K1, P1, K1, P3,
rep from *.
Row 5 *K4, P1, K3, rep from *.

roman stitch

multiple of 2
Rows 1 and 3 (RS) K.
Rows 2 and 4 P.
Row 5 *K1, P1, rep from *.
Row 6 *P1, K1, rep from *.

chevron seed

multiple of 8
Row 1 (RS) *P1, K3, rep from *.
Row 2 *K1, P5, K1, P1, rep from *.
Row 3 *K2, P1, K3, P1, K1,
rep from *.
Row 4 *P2, K1, P1, K1, P3, rep
from *.

basketweave

multiple of 8 plus 4 extra
Row 1 (RS) K4, *P4, K4, rep from *.
Row 2 P4, *K4, P4, rep from *.
Rows 3 and 4 as Rows 1 and 2.
Rows 5 and 7 as Row 2.
Rows 6 and 8 as Row 1.

single twisted rib

multiple of 2
Row 1 (RS) *K1 tbl, P1, rep from *.
Row 2 as Row 1.

farrow rib

multiple of 3
Row 1 and every row *K2, P1,
rep from *.

embossed chevron

multiple of 12

Row 1 (RS) *K3, P5, K3, P1, rep from *.

Row 2 and every alternate row K the K sts and P the P sts as they appear.

Row 3 P1, *K3, P3, rep from * to last 5 sts, K3, P2.

Row 5 P2, *K3, P1, K3, P5, rep from * to last 10 sts, K3, P1, K3, P3.

Row 7 *P3, K5, P3, K1, rep from *.

Row 9 K1, *P3, K3, rep from * to last 5 sts, P3, K2.

Row 11 K2, *P3, K1, P3, K5, rep from * ending last rep K3.

Row 12 as Row 2.

embossed leaf stitch

multiple of 10
Row 1 (RS) K.
Row 2 P.
Rows 3 and 4 K.
Row 5 *P5, K5, rep from *.
Row 6 *P4, K5, P1, rep from *.
Row 7 *K2, P5, K3, rep from *.
Row 8 *P2, K5, P3, rep from *.
Row 9 *K4, P5, K1, rep from *.
Row 10 P.
Row 11 as Row 6.
Row 12 as Row 7.
Row 13 as Row 8.
Row 14 as Row 9.
Row 15 *K5, P5, rep from *.
Row 16 K.

stepped pattern

multiple of 18

Row 1 (RS) *K15, P3, rep from *.

Row 2 and every alternate row K the K sts and P the P sts as they appear.

Row 3 *K15, P3, rep from *.

Rows 5 and 7 *K3, P15, rep from *.

Rows 9 and 11 *K3, P3, K12, rep from *.

Rows 13 and 15 *P6, K3, P9, rep from *.

Rows 17 and 19 *K9, P3, K6, rep from *.

Rows 21 and 23 *P12, K3, P3, rep from *.

Row 24 as Row 2.

woven stitch

multiple of 2
Rows 1 and 3 (WS) P.
Row 2 K1, *sl 1 wyf, K1,
rep from * to last st, K1.
Row 4 K1, *K1, sl 1 wyf,
rep from * to last st, K1.

honeycomb slipstitch

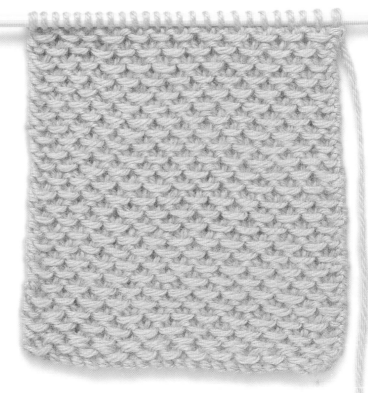

multiple of 2 plus 1 extra
Row 1 (RS) P1, *sl 1 pw, P1,
rep from *.
Rows 2 and 4 P.
Row 3 P2, *sl 1 pw, P1,
rep from * to last st, P1.

knitting
a project

You will sometimes hear people say, 'I can knit and purl, but I can't follow a knitting pattern.' It is true that patterns often look very complex, and to the uninitiated they may even appear to be written in a foreign language. However, it is relatively easy to learn this language, as you will discover.

All but the simplest projects will contain increases, decreases and seams, and many will need you to be able to pick up stitches or make a buttonhole; all of these techniques are shown on the following pages. And, most importantly for a novice knitter, you will learn how to correct any mistakes you may make.

selecting a pattern

First of all, it is important to select a pattern that is appropriate for your level of ability, so that it will be successful and encourage you to develop your knitting skills. If you are choosing your first pattern, try to select something that is not absolutely dependent on perfect sizing and shaping. Also, do not choose a very complicated stitch pattern.

size

Check that the sizes given include one that is suitable for your measurements. It will allow some room for movement when wearing the garment. (This is known as 'ease' or 'tolerance'.) If several sets of figures are given, the smallest one is always indicated first, with larger ones in brackets. It is a good idea to circle each figure that refers to your size.

materials and equipment

A printed pattern will specify all the materials and equipment necessary to complete the garment. It will state the amount and type of yarn, needle sizes, the correct tension/gauge (see page 50), and any haberdashery required, such as buttons or zips.

When you are still learning to knit, it is wise to choose the exact yarn specified in the pattern. Later, when you are more experienced, you can often substitute a different yarn for the one specified. For guidance in buying yarn, see pages 10–13 and 14.

sequence of working

The pattern will indicate the order in which the pieces are to be worked. It is advisable to stick to this order. Often some instructions in one piece will relate to previously completed pieces. It is also advisable to join the pieces together in the order suggested, because this may relate to some further work such as a neckband or collar.

Make it a habit to check your work as you go along, especially if it has a complicated stitch pattern. Lay it out flat in good light and look at it carefully. A check of the number of stitches on the needle will also indicate whether all is going according to plan.

knitting language

All knitting patterns use abbreviations and symbols of various kinds in order to save space. These are fairly standard, although you will find some differences in patterns produced in different English-speaking countries and in different spinners' patterns and knitting books. A full list of the abbreviations used in this book is given on page 6. Special abbreviations are explained at the beginning of a pattern.

In addition to abbreviations, patterns use symbols such as ( ), [ ], and * *. These may contain variations for different sizes, and they may also enclose a set of instructions that are to be repeated.

For example, '*K1, P1, rep from * to end.'
Sections of a pattern that are to be
repeated may use two or more asterisks,
to indicate repeats within repeats.

    You will find, as you gain experience,
that such symbols are easy to understand.

A simple shape, such as
a blanket, can be a good
opportunity to experiment
with colour and texture.

tension/gauge

A most important part of any knitting pattern is the part that states the required tension/gauge. This is the number of stitches and rows, over a given measurement, obtained by the designer of that pattern. It will be given in a form such as: '21 sts and 30 rows to 10 cm (4 in), worked over st st on 4 mm needles'. Sometimes the tension/gauge will be given 'over patt' – that is, over the stitch pattern used for the main part of the garment. It is essential to check your tension/gauge in order for the garment to be the correct size. To do this, you must knit a swatch before beginning the garment itself.

knitting a swatch

1 Cast on a few more stitches than stated by the pattern for the tension/gauge. For example, if 21 stitches are required, you should cast on 28. Work in the pattern, using the specified needles, until the work measures just over 10 cm (4 in), then cast/bind off.

2 Pin the swatch to a flat, padded surface as shown. It is important not to stretch the swatch when pinning it out or your stitch count will not be accurate. In some cases, such as a highly textured or lacy pattern, it may be necessary to block the work (see page 70) in order to make it as smooth as the finished garment will be.

3 Insert a pin, as shown, a few stitches in from one edge. Count off the number of stitches required for the tension/ gauge and insert

another pin. Measure the distance between the pins. It should be 10 cm (4 in) (or the measurement given). If the measurement is greater, your tension/gauge is too loose, and you should change to smaller needles. If it is shorter, your tension/gauge is too tight, and you should change to larger needles.

The row tension/gauge is measured in the same way, although if it is given over stocking/stockinette stitch, you may find it easier to count it on the ridged, purl side of the work. The row tension/gauge is usually less important than the stitch tension/gauge, because shaping instructions (for armholes, neck opening, etc.) are normally given after a certain measurement has been achieved, rather than after a given number of rows. However, some patterns require a given

number of pattern repeats to be completed at certain shaping points, and in such cases if the row tension/gauge varies from that required, the proportions of the garment will be incorrect.

It is a good idea to re-check your tension/gauge during the course of knitting a garment to make sure it has not altered. You can do this on a completed section of the garment.

Do not try to achieve the correct tension/gauge by changing your way of knitting; the tension/gauge with which you knit is natural to you. Change the needle size instead.

Your tension/gauge may vary, however, if you are especially tired or tense, or if you have not done any knitting for a while. In such cases, begin by knitting a few rows with some spare yarn and needles until you resume your natural rhythm.

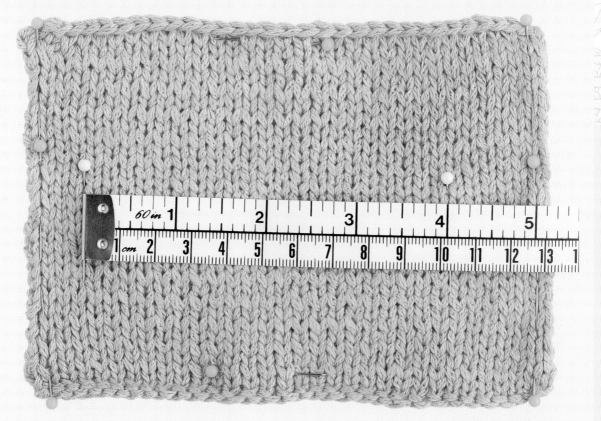

Pinning your swatch correctly
is vital for obtaining the correct
tension/gauge.

complex stitch patterns

It is often confusing to be given
the tension/gauge over a complex
stitch pattern. How do you make a
swatch without casting on all the
stitches required for a section?

Look at the first row that
contains a repeated group of
stitches and calculate how many
stitches are in the repeat. For
example, take these instructions:
'*(K1, P1, K1) into first st, P3

tog, rep from * to end.' When
you have followed the first
instruction, in brackets, you will
have 3 stitches; from the second,
'purl 3 together', you will have
1 stitch. Add the 1 to the 3 to
get the number of stitches in one
repeat: 4.

The number of stitches to cast
on must be divisible by 4 and
include a few stitches more than
those specified for the tension/

gauge. Add any edge stitches
given in the pattern; these will
be found outside the asterisks.
Cast on this number and work
as instructed until the swatch
measures just over 10 cm (4 in).

If the stitches are hard to
count, tie loops of yarn at the
beginning and end of the
specified number of stitches and
rows. Then measure the tension
(gauge) between these markers.

correcting mistakes

Every knitter occasionally makes a mistake, so it is a good idea to learn how to deal effectively with these when they occur.

First of all, keep a crochet hook within easy reach while you are knitting. This is used to pick up dropped stitches. A cable needle is also sometimes useful for holding a loose stitch while you sort out a problem. After correcting a mistake, count the stitches to make sure that you have the right number.

picking up a ladder

If the work is in stocking/ stockinette stitch, insert the crochet hook from front to back through the lowest stitch, pick up the strand as shown, and pull it through to make a new stitch; repeat to the top of the ladder, and place the last stitch on the LH needle, making sure it is turned the correct way for knitting.

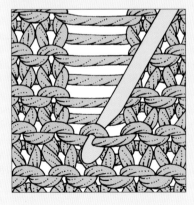

picking up in purl

In some patterns you will need to pick up purl stitches when retrieving a ladder. The technique is basically the same as for a knit stitch, but the hook is inserted from back to front as shown.

unpicking stitches

If you find a mistake a few rows down, it is feasible to unpick the work stitch by stitch until you reach the mistake, then correct it and proceed as usual.

To unpick a knit stitch, put the LH needle through the lower stitch. Pull the RH needle out of the stitch above it, and pull the yarn out of the loop.

To unpick a purl stitch, the process is essentially the same as for a knit stitch, but the yarn is held in front of the work.

unravelling

If the mistake is more than a few rows down, it will be quicker to unravel the work. Unravel it to one or two rows below that in which the mistake occurs, ending with the yarn at the RH edge. In some patterns it is easier to work from the right side of the fabric; in others, including stocking/stockinette stitch, it is easier to work on the wrong (usually purl) side, as shown here.

Insert the needle into the stitch below the RH loop from back to front, and pull out the loop. Continue in this way to the end of the row.

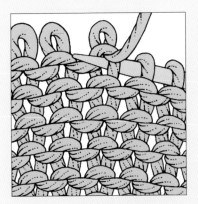

Left-handed knitters may prefer to unravel the work so that the yarn is at the LH edge and then work from left to right if this easier for them.

tip

As a general rule, the amount of yarn needed to knit one row is four times the width of the knitting. More may be required for highly textured patterns.

When picking up stitches after unravelling, use a needle two or three sizes smaller than those used for the knitting. This avoids pulling the stitches out of shape.

For unravelling hairy yarns, keep some sharp-pointed scissors handy to snip any caught-up fibres. Be extra careful, however, not to cut the main strand of yarn. A magnifying glass may prove useful in such cases.

selvedges

A selvedge is a specially worked edge on a piece of knitting. It may be added to give a smooth, firm edge on a fabric, such as stocking/ stockinette stitch, which would otherwise have a rather loose one, and so make the edges easier to handle when seaming. Or it may give a decorative finish to a piece of knitting that will not be seamed – a scarf, for example – and prevent the edges from curling, as some stitch patterns are apt to do.

Patterns rarely include selvedges in the instructions. In the case of a one-stitch selvedge, to be joined in a seam, it is not usually necessary to add extra stitches. However, if the fabric stitch pattern is a complex one, or if there is a detailed colour pattern, such as a traditional Fair Isle motif, you may wish to add a selvedge stitch to each edge, so that the pattern can run smoothly across the seam.

single chain edge

This selvedge gives a smooth edge which is especially appropriate for pieces that will be joined edge to edge (see page 71) or where stitches will be picked up (see page 65).

Right side: slip the first stitch knitwise; knit the last stitch.

Wrong side: slip the first stitch purlwise; purl the last stitch.

single garter edge

This method produces a firm edge on fabrics that tend to be loose, and is especially well suited to seaming with backstitch (see page 72).

Right and wrong sides: knit the first and the last stitch.

double garter edge

This is a decorative edge which lies flat. Allow 2 extra stitches for each edge.

Right and wrong sides: slip the first stitch knitwise and knit the second stitch. At the end of the row, knit the last 2 stitches.

making one purl stitch
This is also abbreviated as 'M 1'.

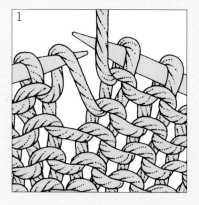

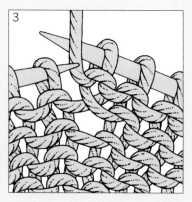

1 Insert the LH needle from front to back under the strand lying between the two adjacent stitches on the LH and RH needles.

2 Purl into the back of the new loop just formed, twisting it as shown to make this possible.

3 Slip the loop off the LH needle.

lifted increase – knitwise
Like the 'M1' increase, this type of increase is inconspicuous.

1 With the RH needle, pull up the stitch lying directly below the next stitch on the LH needle, from front to back, and knit into it.

2 Now knit into the next stitch on the LH needle.

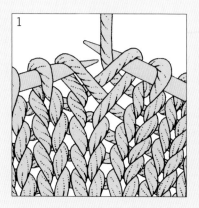

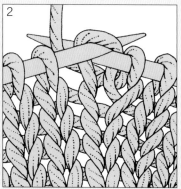

single garter edge

This method produces a firm edge on fabrics that tend to be loose, and is especially well suited to seaming with backstitch (see page 72).

Right and wrong sides: knit the first and the last stitch.

double garter edge

This is a decorative edge which lies flat. Allow 2 extra stitches for each edge.

Right and wrong sides: slip the first stitch knitwise and knit the second stitch. At the end of the row, knit the last 2 stitches.

increases and decreases

There are many different methods of increasing and decreasing, and they are used for many different purposes. A series of increases or decreases may be used at the edge of a piece of knitting or across a row to shape it. Increases and decreases are also used decoratively to produce many interesting stitch patterns. When used for stitch patterns, increases and decreases are normally paired, so that the number of stitches on the needle remains the same. In some lace patterns there will be a temporary increase in the number of stitches, but this will be reduced to the normal number a row or two later.

A 'decorative increase' makes a hole in the fabric and is used mainly in lace patterns. It is produced by taking the yarn over or around the needle. The method varies slightly, depending on the starting position of the yarn, but the effect is the same.

bar increase – knitwise

A bar increase – usually indicated in patterns as 'inc 1' – involves working twice into the same stitch. Whether worked on a knit row or a purl row, this produces a tiny horizontal strand on the knit side of the work. If worked a few stitches in from the edge, it can have a decorative effect.

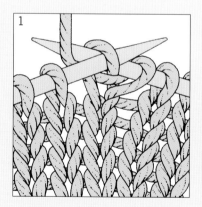

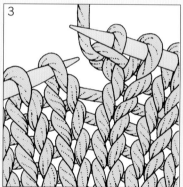

1 Knit into the front of the stitch as usual, but do not slip the stitch off the needle.

2 Now knit again into the same stitch through the back of the loop.

3 Slip the stitch off the LH needle. Two stitches have been made from one. This method of increasing is often used to create fullness above the ribbing – known as a 'mass increase'.

bar increase – purlwise

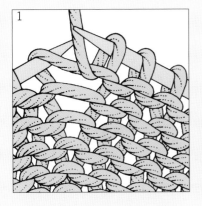

1 Purl the stitch in the usual way, but do not slip the stitch off the needle.

2 Purl again into the same stitch through the back of the loop – twisting the stitch as shown.

3 Slip the stitch off the LH needle. In either a knit or purl bar increase the little bar produced on the knit side will appear to the right of the first of the two stitches. Therefore, if you 'inc 1' into the 4th stitch from the RH edge, you should work across the row until there are 5 stitches remaining, and work the inc 1 into the first of these 5 stitches. On the newly worked row the bar will appear 5 stitches in from each edge.

making one knit stitch
This kind of increase is usually written 'M1'.

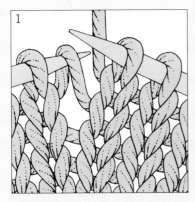

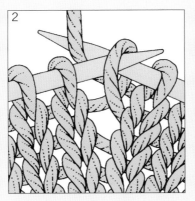

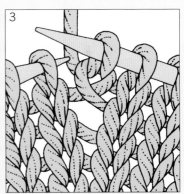

1 Insert LH needle front to back under the strand lying between the two adjacent stitches on the LH and RH needles.

2 Knit into the back of the new loop just formed on the LH needle.

3 Slip the loop off the needle.

making one purl stitch

This is also abbreviated as 'M 1'.

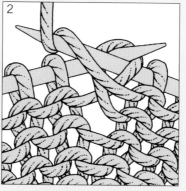

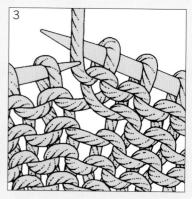

1 Insert the LH needle from front to back under the strand lying between the two adjacent stitches on the LH and RH needles.

2 Purl into the back of the new loop just formed, twisting it as shown to make this possible.

3 Slip the loop off the LH needle.

lifted increase – knitwise

Like the 'M1' increase, this type of increase is inconspicuous.

1 With the RH needle, pull up the stitch lying directly below the next stitch on the LH needle, from front to back, and knit into it.

2 Now knit into the next stitch on the LH needle.

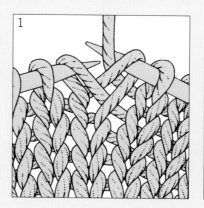

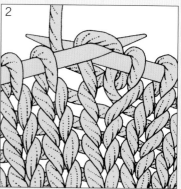

lifted increase – purlwise

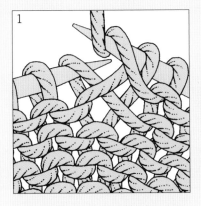

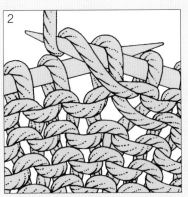

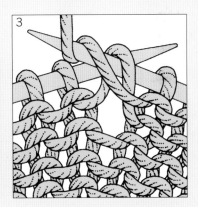

tip

To become familiar with the different effects produced with increases and decreases, cast on about 20 stitches and work in stocking/stockinette stitch using a smooth yarn, practising the techniques shown here.

On each increase/decrease row, attach a little tag identifying the method used. Keep the sample for future reference.

1 With the RH needle, pull up the stitch lying directly below the next stitch on the LH, from back to front, and purl into it.

2 Now purl into the next stitch on the LH needle.

yarn forward
This is worked between two knit stitches.

1 Bring the yarn to the front of the work, then back over the needle.

2 Knit the stitch in the usual way. An extra loop has been formed on the needle.

3 On the next row, purl into this loop as if it were a stitch (or work as given in the pattern).

yarn round needle

This is worked between two purl stitches, or between a knit and a purl stitch. Begin with the yarn at the front of the work.

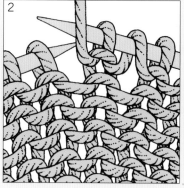

1 Take the yarn over the needle and to the front, thus taking it completely around the needle.

2 Purl the stitch as usual. An extra loop has been formed.

3 On the next row work into this loop as if it were a stitch.

yarn over needle

This is worked between a purl stitch and a knit stitch. The yarn will thus be at the front of the work.

Take the yarn back over the needle. Knit the next stitch in the usual way. On the next row, work into the new loop as instructed by the pattern.

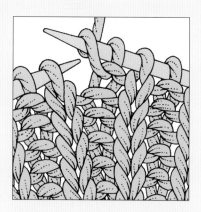

decreasing

There are fewer methods of decreasing than of increasing. Like increases, however, they produce different effects on the fabric and can be employed either inconspicuously or decoratively.

On raglan armholes a decorative type of decreasing – called 'fully fashioned' shaping – is often used. The decreases are worked two stitches in from the edge. At the right-hand edge a slipstitch decrease is worked on the third and fourth stitches from the edge; at the left-hand edge the third and fourth stitches are knitted together.

knitting two stitches together

The instructions for this technique are 'K2 tog'.

 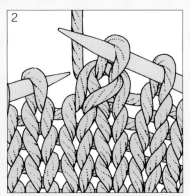

1 Insert the RH needle knitwise into the second stitch on the LH needle and then into the first stitch.

2 Knit the 2 stitches together, and slip the original stitch off the LH needle.

purling two stitches together

The instructions for this technique are 'P2 tog'.

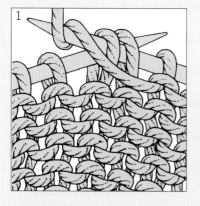

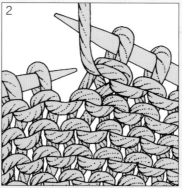

1 Insert the RH needle purlwise into the first stitch on the LH needle and then into the second stitch.

2 Purl the 2 stitches together, and slip the original stitch off the LH needle.

knitting together 'tbl'

When stitches are knitted together normally, they will slant slightly to the right. In some cases a slant to the left will be required. In this case the stitches are knitted through the backs of the loops; the instructions are 'K2 tog tbl'.

Insert the RH needle through the backs of the first and second stitches on the LH needle. Knit the stitches together.

purling together 'tbl'

When stitches are purled together normally, they will slant to the right on the knit side of the work. To achieve a slant to the left, they are purled through the backs of the loops, and the instructions are 'P2 tog tbl'.

Insert the RH needle from back to front through the second stitch and then the first stitch. Purl the two stitches together.

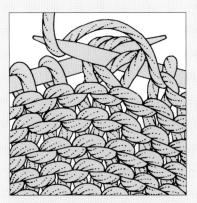

slipstitch decrease – knitwise

Like knitting two together tbl, this produces a distinct slant to the left. Instructions are: 'slip one, knit one, pass slipped stitch over', or 'sl 1, K1, psso' (sometimes 'skpo').

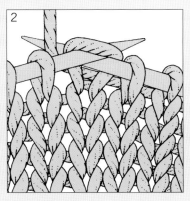

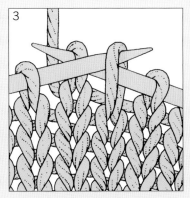

1 Slip the first stitch on the LH needle knitwise.

2 Knit the next stitch.

3 Insert the LH needle into the slipped stitch, and lift it over the knitted stitch.

slipstitch decrease – purlwise

The instructions are: 'slip one, purl one, pass slipped stitch over', or 'sl 1, P1, psso'.

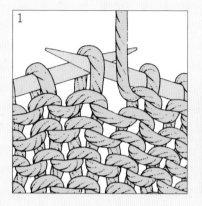

1 With the yarn at the front, slip the first stitch purlwise.

2 Purl the next stitch in the usual way.

3 Insert the LH needle into the slipped stitch and lift it over the purled stitch.

slip, slip, knit decrease

This is similar to an ordinary knitwise slipstitch decrease but produces a smoother effect, which may be preferred in some lace patterns, for example. It is abbreviated 'ssk'.

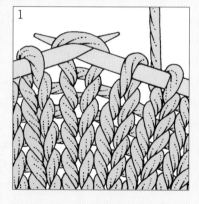

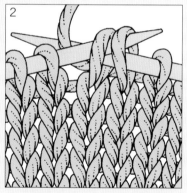

1 Slip the first stitch knitwise, then slip the second knitwise.

2 Insert LH needle into the front of the two slipped stitches, without removing them from the RH; knit them together from the backs of the loops with the RH needle.

picking up stitches

Stitches are often held without being cast/bound off, on a spare needle or stitch holder, and then worked into later after another part of the garment has been completed. For example, the stitches of a pocket lining will not be cast/bound off but held on a spare needle until the pocket is the correct depth and then incorporated into the main section (see page 235).

A double-pointed needle is often the most convenient tool for this purpose, as the stitches can then be worked into from either end. If only a few stitches are to be held, a safety pin or a length of yarn will do. Whether the stitches to be held are knit or purl stitches, always slip them purlwise (see page 27), so that they will be facing the correct way for being worked into.

In some cases, new stitches will need to be picked up from a cast/bound-off edge or side edge; this is called 'K up' or 'pick up and K'. It involves attaching the yarn to the edge and drawing it through the knitting at short intervals. Picking up can be done with either a knitting needle or a crochet hook.

The pattern will specify how many stitches are to be picked up. It is important to space them evenly, which can be tricky on a curved edge. Using large pins, mark the halfway point of the edge, then divide each of these two sections in half. Further subdivisions may sometimes be necessary. Divide the number of stitches to be picked up by the number of sections, and space these groups of stitches accordingly. Count the stitches in each section and then count the total, to make sure you have the required number.

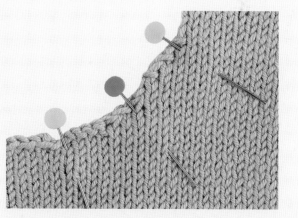

Insert knitter's pins along the curved section of a neckline to facilitate even spacing when picking up stitches.

picking up stitches on a cast/bound-off edge

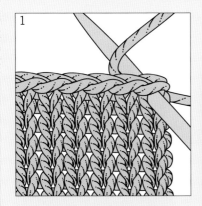

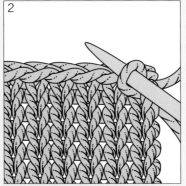

1 Fasten the yarn discreetly just under the RH edge. Insert the needle from front to back through the first edge stitch.

2 Take the yarn under and over the needle to form a loop, and draw the loop through to the front. Repeat to the end. The first row will be worked on the wrong side.

picking up stitches on a side edge

The method is essentially the same as when picking up cast/bound-off stitches. In this case, however, you will probably need to plan the spacing of the stitches, as for a curved edge, since working into every stitch or every other stitch may yield too many or too few. Work one stitch in from the edge, taking care not to encroach on the next line of stitches.

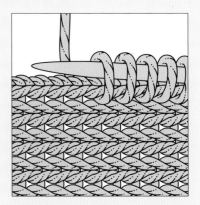

picking up stitches with a crochet hook

1 Fasten the yarn just under the LH edge. Using a crochet hook, pull a loop through to the front of the work.

2 Insert the needle into this loop, and pull the yarn slightly to make it snug. Repeat all along the edge.

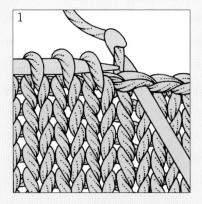

left-handed knitters

Left-handed knitters may prefer to work this method from the wrong side of the work, moving from right to left.

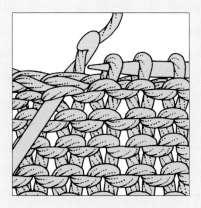

buttonholes

Many garments are fastened with buttons, and therefore making buttonholes is an important skill to learn. Buttonholes are not difficult. The easiest is the eyelet buttonhole; this is used on baby clothes, but is also suitable for some adults' garments. If the knitting is in a medium-weight yarn the hole produced will accommodate a flat button with a diameter of up to 1.5 cm (⅝ in).

Horizontal buttonholes are often worked in a ribbed band, worked on stitches picked up along the centre front edge of a cardigan or jacket, so that the ribs are at a right angle to the jacket and the buttonholes run vertically. A true vertical buttonhole is best used only for purely decorative fastenings, as it is the weakest of the three kinds of buttonhole.

Buttonholes can be strengthened and neatened using the techniques shown on page 241.

horizontal buttonhole

On the right side, work to the position for the buttonhole.

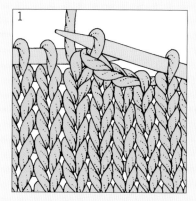

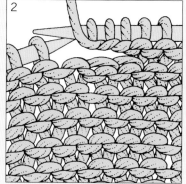

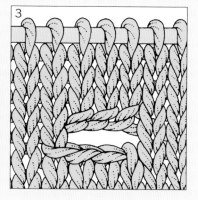

1 Cast/bind off the specified number of stitches. Work to the end.

2 On the wrong side, cast on the same number of stitches as were cast/bound off, using the single cast-on (see page 18).

3 On the next row, work into the back of the cast-on stitches for a neat finished effect.

vertical buttonhole

On the right side, work up to the position of the buttonhole.

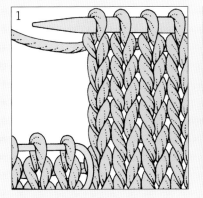

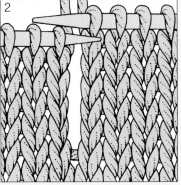

1 Slip the remaining stitches onto a stitch holder. Turn the work and continue on these stitches for the specified number of rows, ending with a right-side row. Do not break off the yarn.

2 Join a new length of yarn to the buttonhole edge of the held stitches. Using the needle in the RH stitches, work to the end, then turn and continue on these stitches until there is one row less than on the RH side.

3 Fasten off the second length of yarn, and continue working to the end of the row. A smoother edge will result if the first stitch on every other row, at the buttonhole edge, is slipped, rather than worked into.

eyelet buttonhole

Work to the position of the buttonhole.

1 Bring the yarn forward (see page 59) to make a new stitch. Insert the needle knitwise into the next 2 stitches.

2 Knit the stitches together to decrease one stitch. On the following row, work into the new loop.

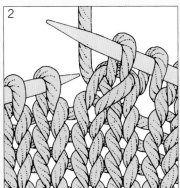

blocking and pressing

After spending hours knitting a garment, it is important not to skimp on the making-up process. Care at this stage will ensure that your knitting is shown to best advantage.

Before joining pieces of knitting, you will need to block them to shape, and possibly press them. The garment pattern instructions will usually specify how the work is to be treated. For blocking or pressing you will need a firm, flat surface padded with a blanket and a sheet or towel; an ironing board can be used for small pieces. You will also need rustproof pins.

wet blocking

Pin the piece right side up to the flat surface, following the measurements given in the pattern. Make sure that the knitting runs straight and that the shape is not distorted. Insert the pins at intervals of 2 cm (¾ in), at an angle through the edge stitch of the knitting into the padding. Do not pin the ribbing.

Dampen the work thoroughly with cool water, using a spray bottle. Leave the knitting to dry completely.

steam blocking

This treatment is suitable for natural fibres. First pin the pieces to the work surface as for wet blocking. To apply steam, use either a steam iron and a dry cloth or a dry iron and a damp cloth. Place the cloth over the work and hold the iron just above it, allowing the steam to penetrate the knitting. Allow the work to dry before removing the pins.

pressing

Pin the pieces wrong side up to the flat surface, using pins with ordinary heads. Do not pin the ribbing. Place the pins close together and insert them diagonally into the padded surface.

Use a steam iron and a dry cloth. For natural-synthetic blends use a dry, cool iron over a dry cloth. Do *not* slide the iron over the surface; instead, place it lightly on one area for a second, then lift it off. Allow the work to cool before taking it off the board.

Pin the piece carefully so that the knitting runs straight.

seams

There are several different ways of joining pieces of knitting, suitable for different parts of a garment. An edge-to-edge seam, for example, is ideal for joining a buttonhole band to a front edge as there is little bulk and the seam is almost invisible. Backstitch is the preferred method where strength is required – as in a side seam. Some edges may be grafted, rather than sewn together; for this advanced technique see page 226.

    The yarn used for knitting the garment can be used for the sewing. However, if this yarn is a chunky weight, you should work with a lighter-weight yarn. Always fasten the yarn with a couple of backstitches.

edge-to-edge seam

This seaming stitch is also known as mattress stitch.
Place both pieces right side up on a flat surface.

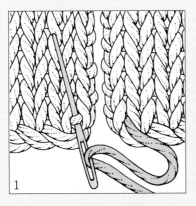 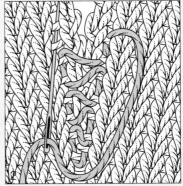

1 Fasten the yarn to the wrong side, on the RH edge, and bring it to the right side between the edge stitch and the next stitch on the first row of knitting.

2 Take it across and under the stitch loop between the edge stitch and the next stitch on the first row on the LH edge; draw the edges together, then work between the edge stitch and the next stitch on the second row on the RH edge. Continue along the seam, pulling the yarn to bring the edges smoothly together.

backstitch seam
Pin the two pieces together with right sides facing.

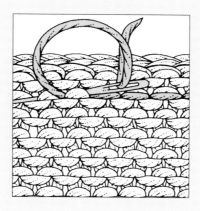

Fasten the yarn at the RH corner. Work from right to left, taking the yarn across two stitches on the under side, then back over one stitch on top, so that the stitches meet end to end as shown. On the other side, the stitches overlap.

setting in a sleeve
A sleeve with a curved sleeve head is set into the armhole after joining the adjacent seams.

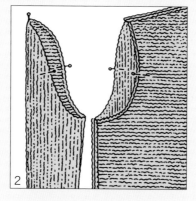

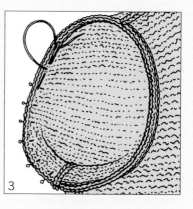

1 Turn the main part of the garment wrong side out. Insert a pin into the front and back edges halfway between the two seams. Turn the sleeve right side out, and insert pins at the centre point and halfway down.

2 Position the sleeve inside the armhole, and pin the edges together, matching the pins and seams. Add more pins around the edge, placing them about 2–3 cm (¾–1 in) apart and easing the sleeve to fit the armhole, if necessary. You may wish to tack/baste the edges together.

3 Work around the armhole, about 5 mm (¼ in) from the edge, using backstitch and working from the sleeve side.

darning in ends

Yarn ends left from knitting or seaming should be darned into the work, usually along the edge. Use a tapestry needle, to avoid splitting the stitches. Work a small stitch in the edge, then take the yarn through the edge stitches for a short distance and cut it off. For extra security, take it back in the opposite direction, as shown. If the yarn is too thick for the needle eye or too short to manipulate, use a crochet hook to pull it through the stitches.

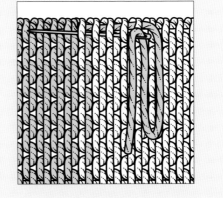

darning in ends in a motif

In intarsia knitting (see page 164), where a motif is completed, two lengths of yarn will be left: one from the motif and one from the background. (The remaining background colour is used to continue the knitting.) Cut these two ends, leaving enough for the darning (it need not go all the way around a motif unless the difference in thickness would be visible on the right side). Weave the ends through the edge of the motif, making sure that the darker yarn does not show through the lighter knitting.

knitting a project
complex textures

These patterns suggest the infinite possibilities available through the techniques of increasing and decreasing. Daisy stitch and coral knit stitch illustrate textures that can be achieved by alternately increasing and then decreasing the stitches that make up the fabric. Nut pattern employs basically the same principle to form little clusters and resembles the bobble patterns shown on pages 120–125.

Leaf and chevron patterns are examples of linear effects formed through increases and decreases. In chevron the downward points are formed by decreasing, the upward ones by increasing. The pointed/scalloped edge of these patterns is less apparent when worked above ribbing.

In fisherman's rib the stitches are not increased, but a technique similar to a lifted increase is used to create a softly elastic texture.

nut pattern

multiple of 4

Row 1 (RS) *P3, (K1, yf, K1) into next st, rep from *.

Rows 2 and 3 *P3, K3, rep from *.

Row 4 *P3 tog, K3, rep from *.

Row 5 P.

Row 6 K.

Row 7 *P1, (K1, yf, K1) into next st, P2, rep from *.

Row 8 K2, *P3, K3, rep from * to last 4 sts, P3, K1.

Row 9 P1, *K3, P3, rep from * to last 5 sts, K3, P2.

Row 10 K2, *P3 tog, K3, rep from * to last 4 sts, P3 tog, K1.

Row 11 P.

Row 12 K.

coral knot stitch

multiple of 2 plus 2 extra
Row 1 (RS) K1, *K2 tog, rep from * to last st, K1.
Row 2 K1, *K1, pick up strand between this and next st and K it, rep from * to last st, K1.
Row 3 K.
Row 4 P.

fisherman's rib

multiple of 2
Row 1 P.
Row 2 *P1, K next st in the row
below, rep from * to last 2 sts, P2.
Rep Row 2 throughout.

leaf pattern

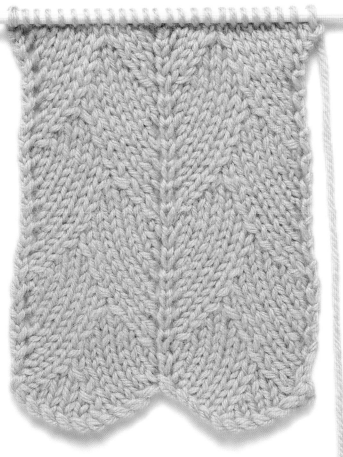

multiple of 24 plus 1 extra

Note 'K up 1': Pick up a stitch
(see page 65).

Row 1 (RS) K1, *K up 1, sl 1, K1,
psso, K4, K2 tog, K3, K up 1, K1,
K up 1, K3, sl 1, K1, psso, K4,
K2 tog, K up 1, K1, rep from *.

Row 2 and every alternate row P.

Row 3 K1, *K up 1, K1, sl 1, K1,
psso, K2, K2 tog, K4, K up 1, K1,
K up 1, K4, sl 1, K1, psso, K2,
K2 tog, K1, K up 1, K1, rep from *.

Row 5 K1, *K up 1, K2, sl 1, K1,
psso, K2 tog, K5, K up 1, K1,
K up 1, K5, sl 1, K1, psso, K2 tog,
K2, K up 1, K1, rep from *.

Row 7 K1, *K up 1, K3, sl 1, K1,
psso, K4, K2 tog, K up 1, K1,
K up 1, sl 1, K1, psso, K4, K2 tog,
K3, K up 1, K1, rep from *.

Row 9 K1, *K up 1, K4, sl 1, K1,
psso, K2, K2 tog, K1, K up 1, K1,
K up 1, K1, sl 1, K1, psso, K2,
K2 tog, K4, K up 1, K1, rep from *.

Row 11 K1, *K up 1, K5, sl 1, K1,
psso, K2 tog, K2, K up 1, K1,
K up 1, K2, sl 1, K1, psso, K2 tog,
K5, K up 1, K1, rep from *.

Row 12 as Row 2.

daisy stitch

multiple of 4 plus 1 extra
Rows 1 and 3 (RS) K.
Row 2 K1, *P3 tog, yon, P same 3 sts tog again, K1, rep from *.
Row 4 K1, P1, K1, *P3 tog, yon, P same 3 sts tog again, K1, rep from * to last 2 sts, P1, K1.

chevron

multiple of 13 plus 2 extra
Row 1 (RS) *K2, M1, K4, sl 1, K2 tog, psso, K4, M1, rep from * to last 2 sts, K2.
Row 2 P.

knitting a project
lace patterns

For many people lace patterns are the most tempting of all types of knitting. The complementary relationship of the knitted fabric itself and the pattern of holes is especially pleasing.

The character of a lace pattern can change quite dramatically, depending on the yarn it is worked in. Try some of the patterns shown in several different yarns: fine baby yarns, soft mohair blends, crisp cotton yarns, glitter yarns. As a general rule, however, the yarn should not be too thick.

If you are beginning a lace pattern at the edge, without any ribbing, it is best to use the single cast-on (see page 18), which produces a soft edge.

snowdrop lace

multiple of 8 plus 5 extra
Rows 1 and 3 (RS) K1, *yf, sl 1 pw, K2 tog, psso, yf, K5, rep from * to last 4 sts, yf, sl 1 pw, K2 tog, psso, yf, K1.
Row 2 and every alternate row P.
Row 5 K1, *K3, yf, sl 1, K1, psso, K1, K2 tog, yf, rep from * to last 4 sts, K4.
Row 7 K1, *yf, sl 1, K2 tog, psso, yf, K1, rep from * to end.
Row 8 as Row 2.

vine lace

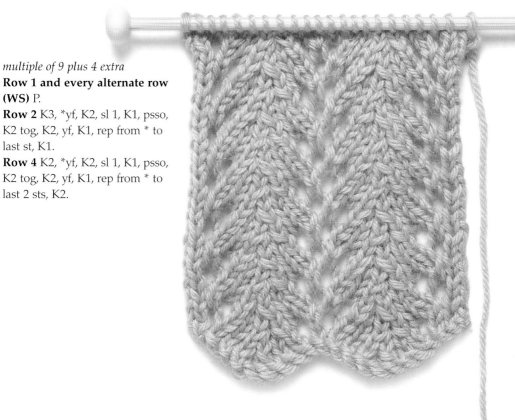

multiple of 9 plus 4 extra

Row 1 and every alternate row (WS) P.

Row 2 K3, *yf, K2, sl 1, K1, psso, K2 tog, K2, yf, K1, rep from * to last st, K1.

Row 4 K2, *yf, K2, sl 1, K1, psso, K2 tog, K2, yf, K1, rep from * to last 2 sts, K2.

quatrefoil eyelet

multiple of 8

Row 1 and every alternate row (WS) P.

Row 2 K.

Row 4 K3, *yf, sl 1, K1, psso, K6, rep from *ending last rep K3 instead of K6.

Row 6 K1, *K2 tog, yf, K1, yf, sl 1, K1, psso, K3, rep from * ending last rep K2 instead of K3.

Row 8 as Row 4.

Row 10 K.

Row 12 K7, *yf, sl 1, K1, psso, K6, rep from * to last st, K1.

Row 14 K5, *K2 tog, yf, K1, yf, sl 1, K1, psso, K3, rep from * to last 3 sts, K3.

Row 16 as Row 12.

chevron lace

multiple of 8 plus 1 extra (multiple is increased 1 st in Row 9, reduced in Row 11)

Row 1 (RS) *K5, yf, K2 tog, K1, rep from * to last st, K1.

Row 2 and every alternate row P.

Row 3 *K3, K2 tog tbl, yf, K1, yf, K2 tog, rep from * to last st, K1.

Row 5 K1, *K1, K2 tog tbl, yf, K3, yf, K2 tog, rep from *.

Row 7 K1, K2 tog tbl, * yf, K5, yf, K2 tog tbl, return st to LH needle, pass next st over it and put st back on RH needle, rep from * to last 6 sts, yf, K6.

Row 9 *K1, K into front and back of next st, K6, rep from * to last st, K1.

Row 11 *K2 tog, K4, yf, K2 tog, K1, rep from * to last st, K1.

Row 12 P.

vandyke stitch

multiple of 10
Row 1 (RS) *yf, sl 1, K1, psso, K8,
rep from *.
**Row 2 and every alternate
row** P.
Row 3 *K1, yf, sl 1, K1, psso, K5,
K2 tog, yf, rep from * ending last
rep K2 not K2 tog, yf.
Row 5 *K2, yf, sl 1, K1, psso, K3,
K2 tog, yf, K1, rep from *.
Row 7 *K5, yf, sl 1, K1, psso, K3,
rep from *.
Row 9 *K3, K2 tog, yf, K1, yf, sl 1,
K1, psso, K2, rep from *.
Row 11 *K2, K2 tog, yf, K3, yf,
sl 1, K1, psso, K1, rep from *.
Row 12 P.

openwork diamond pattern

multiple of 10 plus 2 extra

Row 1 (RS) K1, *K1, yf, sl 1, K1, psso, K5, K2 tog, yf, rep from * to last st, K1.

Row 2 and every alternate row P.

Row 3 K1, *K2, yf, sl 1, K1, psso, K3, K2 tog, yf, K1, rep from * to last st, K1.

Row 5 K1, *K1, (yf, sl 1, K1, psso) twice, K1, (K2 tog, yf) twice, rep from * to last st, K1.

Row 7 K1, *K2, yf, sl 1, K1, psso, yf, sl 1, K2 tog, psso, yf, K2 tog, yf, K1, rep from * to last st, K1.

Row 9 K1, *K3, K2 tog, yf, K1, yf, sl 1, K1, psso, K2, rep from * to last st, K1.

Row 11 K1, *K2, K2 tog, yf, K3, yf, sl 1, K1, psso, K1, rep from * to last st, K1.

Row 13 K1, *K1, (K2 tog, yf) twice, K1, (yf, sl 1, K1, psso) twice, rep from * to last st, K1.

Row 15 K2 tog, *yf, sl 1, K1, psso, yf, K5, yf, sl 1, K1, psso, return st to LH needle, pass next st over it and put st back on RH needle, rep from * to last 10 sts, yf, sl 1, K1, psso, yf, K5, yf, K2 tog, K1.

Row 16 P.

fern lace

multiple of 10 plus 1 extra

Row 1 and every alternate row (WS) P.

Row 2 K3, *K2 tog, yf, K1, yf, sl 1, K1, psso, K5, rep from *ending last rep K3.

Row 4 K2, *K2 tog, (K1, yf) twice, K1, sl 1, K1, psso, K3, rep from * ending last rep K2.

Row 6 K1, *K2 tog, K2, yf, K1, yf, K2, sl 1, K1, psso, K1, rep from *.

Row 8 K2 tog, *K3, yf, K1, yf, K3, sl 1, K2 tog, psso, rep from * to last 9 sts, K3, yf, K1, yf, K3, sl 1, K1, psso.

Row 10 K1, *yf, sl 1, K1, psso, K5, K2 tog, yf, K1, rep from *.

Row 12 K1, *yf, K1, sl 1, K1, psso, K3, K2 tog, K1, yf, K1, rep from *.

Row 14 K1, *yf, K2, sl 1, K1, psso, K1, K2 tog, K2, yf, K1, rep from *.

Row 16 K1, *yf, K3, sl 1, K2 tog, psso, K3, yf, K1, rep from *.

curving lattice lace

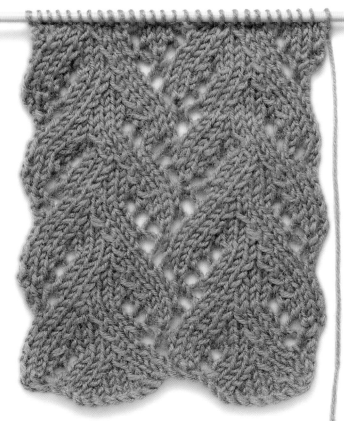

multiple of 13 plus 2 extra

Row 1 (RS) K1, *K2, sl 1, K1, psso, K4, K2 tog, K2, yf, K1, yf, rep from * to last st, K1.

Row 2 and every alternate row P.

Row 3 K1, *yf, K2, sl 1, K1, psso, K2, K2 tog, K2, yf, K3, rep from * to last st, K1.

Row 5 K1, *K1, yf, K2, sl 1, K1, psso, K2 tog, K2, yf, K4, rep from * to last st, K1.

Row 7 K1,*yf, K1, yf, K2, sl 1, K1, psso, K4, K2 tog, K2, rep from * to last st, K1.

Row 9 K1, *K3, yf, K2, sl 1, K1, psso, K2, K2 tog, K2, yf, rep from * to last st, Kl.

Row 11 K1, * K4, yf, K2, sl 1, K1, psso, K2 tog, K2, yf, K1, rep from * to last st, K1.

Row 12 P.

open chevron lace

multiple of 12 plus 1 extra

Row 1 and every alternate row (WS) P.

Row 2 K4, *K2 tog, yf, K1, yf, sl 1, K1, psso, K7, rep from * ending last rep K4.

Row 4 K3, *K2 tog, yf, K3, yf, sl 1, K1, psso, K5, rep from * ending last rep K3.

Row 6 K2, *(K2 tog, yf) twice, K1 , (yf, sl 1, K1, psso) twice, K3, rep from * ending last rep K2.

Row 8 K1, *(K2 tog, yf) twice, K3, (yf, sl 1, K1, psso) twice, K1, rep from *.

Row 10 K2 tog, *yf, K2 tog, yf, K5, yf, sl 1, K1, psso, yf, sl 1, K2 tog, psso, rep from * ending last rep sl 1, K1, psso.

Row 12 K1, *K2 tog, yf, K1, yf, sl 1, K1, psso, K1, rep from *.

Row 14 K2 tog, *yf, K3, yf, sl 1, K2 tog, psso, rep from *ending last rep sl 1, K1, psso.

english mesh lace

multiple of 6 plus 1 extra

Row 1 and every alternate row (WS) P.

Row 2 K1, *yf, sl 1, K1, psso, K1, K2 tog, yf, K1, rep from *.

Row 4 K1 *yf, K1, sl 1, K2 tog, psso, K1, yf, K1, rep from *.

Row 6 K1, *K2 tog, yf, K1, yf, sl 1, K1, psso, K1, rep from *.

Row 8 K2 tog, *(K1, yf) twice, K1, sl 1, K2 tog, psso, rep from * to last 5 sts, (K1, yf) twice, K1, ssk.

falling leaf pattern

multiple of 10 plus 1 extra

Row 1 (RS) K1, *yf, K3, sl 1, K2 tog, psso, K3, yf, K1, rep from *.

Row 2 and every alternate row P.

Row 3 K1, *K1, yf, K2, sl 1, K2 tog, psso, K2, yf, K2, rep from *.

Row 5 K1, *K2, yf, K1, sl 1, K2 tog, psso, K1, yf, K3, rep from *.

Row 7 K1, *K3, yf, sl 1, K2 tog, psso, yf, K4, rep from *.

Row 9 K2 tog, *K3, yf, K1, yf, K3, sl 1, K2 tog, psso, rep from * to last 9 sts, K3, yf, K1, yf, K3, sl 1, K1, psso.

Row 11 K2 tog, *K2, yf, K3, yf, K2, sl 1, K2 tog, psso, rep from * to last 9 sts, K2, yf, K3, yf, K2, sl 1, K1, psso.

Row 13 K2 tog, *K1, yf, K5, yf, K1, sl 1, K2 tog, psso, rep from * to last 9 sts, K1, yf, K5, yf, K1, sl 1, K1, psso.

Row 15 K2 tog, *yf, K7, yf, sl 1, K2 tog, psso, rep from * to last 9 sts, yf, K7, yf, sl 1, K1, psso.

Row 16 P.

fishtail lace

multiple of 10 plus 1 extra
Row 1 (RS) K1, *yf, K3, sl 1, K2 tog, psso, K3, yf, K1, rep from *.
Row 2 and every alternate row P.
Row 3 K1, *K1, yf, K2, sl 1, K2 tog, psso, K2, yf, K2, rep from *.
Row 5 K1, *K2, yf, K1, sl 1, K2 tog, psso, K1, yf, K3, rep from *.
Row 7 K1, *K3, yf, sl 1, K2 tog, psso, yf, K4, rep from *.
Row 8 P.

special textures

Once you have mastered the basic knitting skills and can follow a pattern, why not try some more adventurous stitch patterns? The techniques described here require some facility in handling yarn and needles, but the fascinating results are well worth the effort. With only a little practice you can produce gracefully coiling cables, large and small bobbles, knitted smocking and shaggy looped pile fabrics. The versatility of knitting is amply demonstrated in these pages.

It is well worth experimenting with different yarns to see how many varied effects are possible using these stitches. For example, cables are often worked in Aran yarn, as part of a traditional Aran-style sweater; but they can look especially beautiful in a glossy cotton or silk yarn, and they also lend themselves well to mohair and angora yarns. Bobbles are normally worked in smooth yarns, such as wool double-knitting; in cotton they have a crisper texture.

twisted stitches and cables

Some of the most beautiful of all stitch patterns involve crossing stitches over each other. Stitches can be crossed in many different ways. Some crossing techniques are worked entirely on the main pair of needles; these are often referred to as 'twisting' the stitches. Up to four stitches can be twisted on the two needles, to produce mock cables which are virtually indistinguishable from those produced with a cable needle.

It is important, when twisting stitches, to keep a loose tension/gauge on the twist row and on those preceding and following it. This makes the work easier and reduces strain on the yarn. When cabling, always use a cable needle no larger than the main needles, to avoid distorting the stitches.

Cables may coil either to the right – called 'cable back' – or to the left – called 'cable forward'. The basic cable can be worked over 4, 6 or 8 stitches.

Different effects are achieved by varying the number of rows between cable rows, though the same technique is used whatever the number. Working the cable every sixth row produces a graceful coil; on every fourth row, a thick, rope-like effect; on every tenth or twelfth row, a flat effect like a twisted ribbon. A novel effect can be produced by using a contrasting colour for half of the cable stitches.

variations on cabling

The basic cable technique can be used to move a single stitch or a group of stitches across the fabric, forming more complex cable and lattice patterns. The illustrations on page 103 show how to move a single knit stitch to the right or the left on a background of reverse stocking/ stockinette stitch. The same basic method can be used to move different numbers of stitches at a time. To become familiar with cabling techniques, make a sample, using Aran or double-knitting yarn.

Twisted stitches and cable are shown in this sample. At left, two stitches have been twisted right on every fourth row. At right, a 'cable 4 forward' has been worked on every sixth row.

twist 2 right
(abbreviated Tw2R)

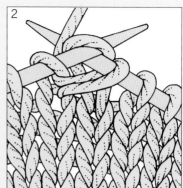

1 Take the RH needle in front of the first stitch on the LH needle and knit into the second stitch. Do not let the first stitch slip off the needle.

2 Knit into the first stitch and slip both stitches off the LH needle. On the next row, purl into the twisted stitches as usual. The stitches twist to the right.

twist 2 left
(abbreviated Tw2L)

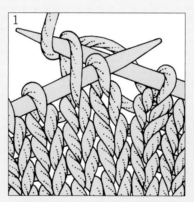

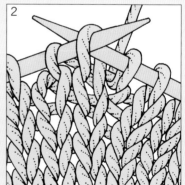

1 Take the RH needle behind the first stitch on the LH needle, and knit into the second stitch through the back of the loop.

2 Knit into the first stitch, also through the back of the loop. On the next row, purl into the twisted stitches as usual. The stitches now twist to the left.

twist 2 right purlwise
(abbreviated Tw2PR)

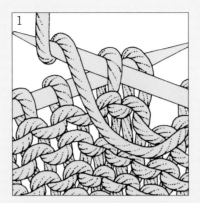

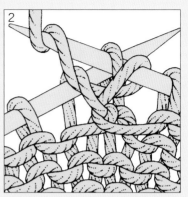

1 Take the RH needle in front of the first stitch on the LH needle and purl into the second stitch.

2 Purl into the first stitch. Slip both stitches off the LH needle. On the next row, knit into the twisted stitches as usual. The stitches twist to the right on the knit side of the work.

twist 2 left purlwise
(abbreviated Tw2PL)

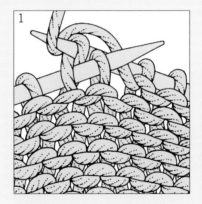

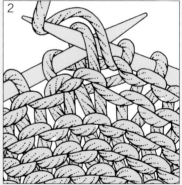

1 Take the RH needle and yarn behind the first stitch on the LH needle, and purl into the back of the second stitch, twisting it as shown. Take care not to let the first stitch slip off the needle.

2 Purl into the front of the first stitch, and let both stitches slip off the needle. On the next row, knit into the twisted stitches as usual. The stitches twist to the left on the knit side of the work.

mock cable back

This mock cable contains
4 stitches.

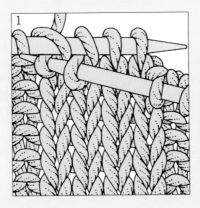

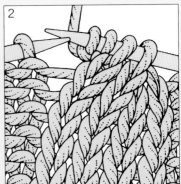

1 Take the RH needle in front of
the first 2 stitches and knit the
third stitch. Knit the fourth
stitch. Leave all 4 stitches on
the LH needle. Knit the second
stitch on the LH needle.

2 Knit the first stitch. Slip all
4 stitches off the needle.
On the following row, purl
these stitches, remembering
to keep the tension/gauge
fairly loose. The resulting
cable twists to the right.

mock cable forward

For this mock cable, knit the
third and fourth stitches through
the back of the loops. Then knit
the first stitch through the front
in the usual way, slip it off the
needle, knit the second stitch
through the front and slip all
stitches off the needle.

The resulting cable twists to
the left.

knot – method 1

This small bobble, or knot, is produced in essentially the same way as the Method 1 bobble on page 104, but the increased stitches are immediately decreased.

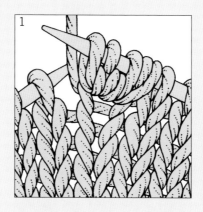

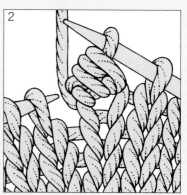

1 Knit, purl, knit, purl and knit into the stitch, thus making 5 stitches out of one.

2 With the LH needle, lift the second, third, fourth and fifth stitches over the first one, thus decreasing back to one stitch and completing the knot.

knot – method 2

This method produces a slightly flatter and smoother knot than Method 1, above.

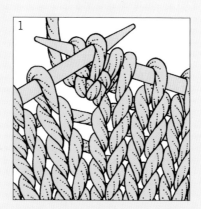

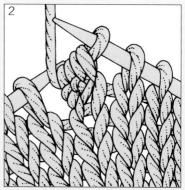

1 Knit into the front, back, front and back of the stitch, thus making 4 stitches out of one. With the LH needle, lift the second stitch over the first one.

2 Lift the third and fourth stitches over the first one, completing the knot.

mock cable back

This mock cable contains
4 stitches.

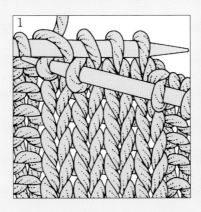

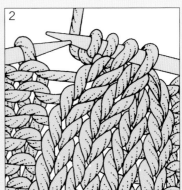

1 Take the RH needle in front of
the first 2 stitches and knit the
third stitch. Knit the fourth
stitch. Leave all 4 stitches on
the LH needle. Knit the second
stitch on the LH needle.

2 Knit the first stitch. Slip all
4 stitches off the needle.
On the following row, purl
these stitches, remembering
to keep the tension/gauge
fairly loose. The resulting
cable twists to the right.

mock cable forward

For this mock cable, knit the
third and fourth stitches through
the back of the loops. Then knit
the first stitch through the front
in the usual way, slip it off the
needle, knit the second stitch
through the front and slip all
stitches off the needle.

The resulting cable twists to
the left.

cable 6 back
(abbreviated C6B)

1 Work to the position of the cable, slip the next 3 stitches onto the cable needle and hold them at the back of the work. Knit the next 3 stitches.

2 Knit the 3 stitches from the cable needle. On the next row, purl these stitches as usual. The cable coils to the right.

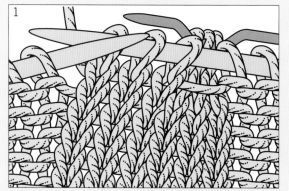

cable 6 forward
(abbreviated C6F)

1 Work to the position of the cable, slip the next 3 stitches onto the cable needle and hold them at the front of the work. Knit the next 3 stitches.

2 Knit the 3 stitches from the cable needle. On the next row, purl these stitches as usual. The cable coils to the left.

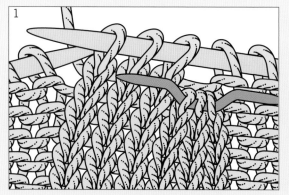

cross 2 back
(abbreviated Cr2B)

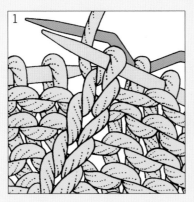

1 Slip the purl stitch immediately before the knit stitch onto a cable needle and hold it at the back of the work. Knit the knit stitch.

2 Purl the stitch from the cable needle.

cross 2 forward
(abbreviated Cr2F)

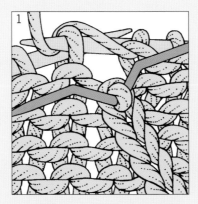

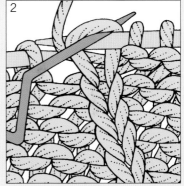

1 Slip the knit stitch onto the cable needle and hold it at the front of the work. Purl the purl stitch.

2 Knit the stitch from the cable needle.

bobbles and knots

Many different sizes and shapes of bobble can be produced, but they are all based on the same principle: making several stitches out of one stitch and then decreasing back to a single stitch, usually after working one or more rows on the increased stitches. The extra rows are usually worked on the bobble alone; this produces a bobble that stands out firmly from the background fabric, being attached to it only at the top and the bottom. A softer bobble is produced by working the increased stitches along with the background fabric. Small bobbles – often called knots – are made by immediately decreasing the increased stitches.

The initial increasing for a bobble can be worked in a variety of ways: by alternately knitting and purling into the stitch, by knitting into the front and back of the stitch alternately, or by taking the yarn over the needle between knit stitches.

bobble – method 1

This bobble is worked in reverse stocking/stockinette stitch and is shown on a stocking stitch fabric. For a stocking/stockinette stitch bobble, reverse the 'knit' and 'purl' instructions in steps 2 and 3.

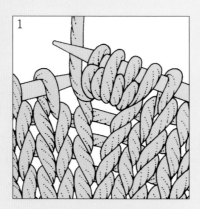

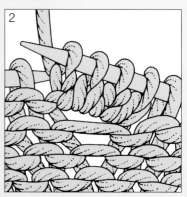

1 Knit, purl, knit and purl into the same stitch, thus making 4 stitches out of one. Turn the work.

2 Knit these 4 stitches. Turn. Purl the stitches. Turn.

3 Repeat step 2 once more. The right (purl) side of the bobble is facing.

4 With the LH needle, lift the second, third and fourth stitches over the first, thus decreasing back to one stitch and completing the bobble.

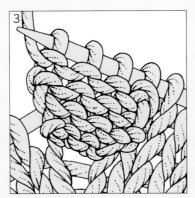

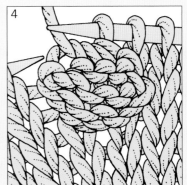

bobble – method 2

This bobble is slightly flatter than that shown in Method 1.

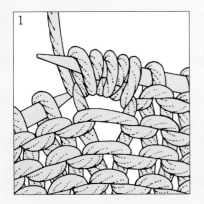

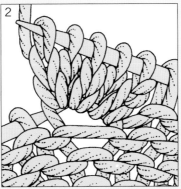

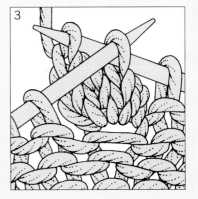

1 Knit 1, yarn forward, knit 1, yarn forward, knit 1. Turn. Purl the stitches. Turn.

2 Knit the stitches. Turn. Purl 2 together, purl 1, purl 2 together: 3 stitches. Turn.

3 Slip 1, knit 2 together, pass the slipped stitch over.

knot – method 1

This small bobble, or knot, is produced in essentially the same way as the Method 1 bobble on page 104, but the increased stitches are immediately decreased.

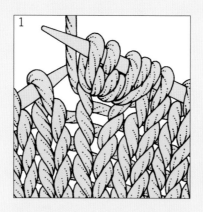 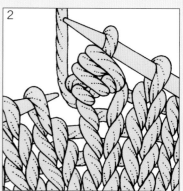

1 Knit, purl, knit, purl and knit into the stitch, thus making 5 stitches out of one.

2 With the LH needle, lift the second, third, fourth and fifth stitches over the first one, thus decreasing back to one stitch and completing the knot.

knot – method 2

This method produces a slightly flatter and smoother knot than Method 1, above.

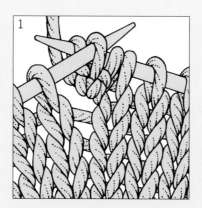

1 Knit into the front, back, front and back of the stitch, thus making 4 stitches out of one. With the LH needle, lift the second stitch over the first one.

2 Lift the third and fourth stitches over the first one, completing the knot.

contrasting bobbles and knots

To work a bobble or knot in a contrasting colour, simply tie the new colour to the first colour at the position for the bobble on the wrong side of the work, drop the first colour and work the bobble in the new colour. When the bobble is completed, break off the yarn and tie the ends together securely. When the knitting is completed, darn the ends into the wrong side. If a series of bobbles is to be worked across a row at short intervals, it may be preferable to weave in the contrasting yarn as shown on page 168.

Bobbles can be worked in as many different colours as you like.

elongated stitches

A variety of openwork effects can be achieved by winding the yarn two or more times around the needle, then, on the following row, working into only the first of each pair or group of loops, allowing the extra loops to unwind. The patterns using this technique – called 'dropped-stitch patterns' – range from simple bands of openwork, formed by elongating the stitches all the way across the fabric – to quite complex patterns.

basic elongated stitch

 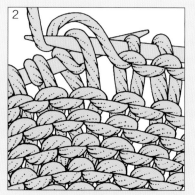

1 Insert the RH needle knitwise into the stitch, take the yarn twice around the needle, and draw the 2 loops through the stitch, allowing it to slip off the needle. Repeat to the end of the row.

2 On the following row, purl into the first of each pair of loops and allow the extra loop to drop off the needle. Either the knit side or the purl side can be used as the right side of the work. Longer stitches can be produced by winding the yarn 3 or more times around the needle.

smocking

A smocked fabric can be produced either by sewing a knitted fabric in a pattern (see page 209) or by knitting in the smocking as you go. The latter method, which is shown here, is based on a rib pattern, which can be varied by adjusting the thickness and/or spacing of the ribs. A cable needle is used to group stitches together so that they can be wrapped with the yarn. The grouped stitches can be wrapped before they are worked, as shown here, or worked first and then wrapped.

Basic ribbed smocking

Cast on a multiple of 8 stitches plus 10. Work in K2, P2 rib for 5 rows. On the 6th (right side) row, work the smocking, as follows:

1 Purl the first 2 (purl) stitches.

2 Slip the next 6 stitches onto the cable needle; hold them at front.

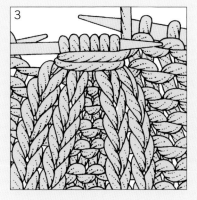

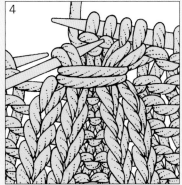

3 Wind the yarn twice around these stitches from left to right, pulling it firmly.

4 Knit 2, purl 2, knit 2 from the cable needle.

5 Repeat steps 1–4 to the end.

6 Work in rib for 5 rows.

7 On the 12th row purl the first 2 stitches.

8 Slip 2 knit stitches onto the cable needle. Wind the yarn around these stitches twice, knit them, then slip them off the cable needle.

9 Purl 2 stitches, repeat steps 2–4 to the last 2 stitches; knit 2. These 12 rows form the pattern.

loop stitch

It is possible to produce looped pile or shaggy fabrics in knitting by winding the yarn around the thumb at regular close intervals. The loops produced in this way can be left as they are, or they can be cut for a shaggy effect.

Loop stitch is easier to work if the yarn is held in the right hand, as shown on page 22. (Left-handed knitters should reverse the movements shown here.)

working loop stitch
Begin by working 2 rows of stocking/stockinette stitch, then knit one or two stitches for the selvedge.

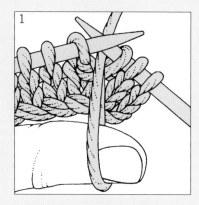

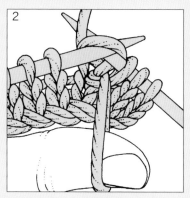

1 Knit the next stitch, but do not let the original stitch slip off the needle. Bring the yarn forward between the needles and take it under the left thumb from back to front, making a loop of the desired length. The length of the loop can be increased by holding the thumb lower.

2 Knit again into the same stitch, and slip the original stitch off the LH needle, still keeping the thumb in the loop.

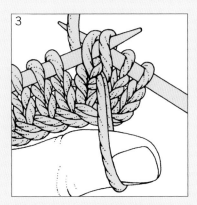

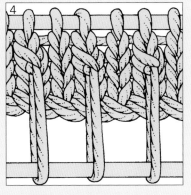

3 With the thumb still in the loop, insert the LH needle through the front of the 2 stitches just made, and knit both stitches together through the back. Slip the thumb out of the loop. Work to the position of the next loop, then repeat steps 1–3. In the drawing the loops are shown separated by a single knit stitch. They may be more widely spaced if desired.

4 Purl the next row. Slip the free needle through the loops, and pull them gently downwards.

Loop stitch (right) has been worked on this fabric in a staggered pattern.

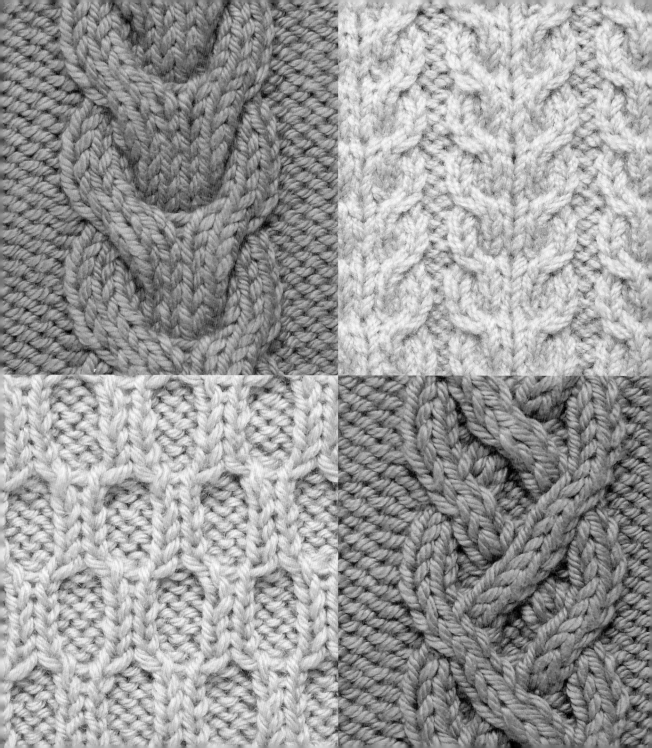

special textures
cable patterns

This selection of cable patterns suggests the rich variety of effects possible when crossing stitches with a cable needle. These samples have been worked in Aran-weight yarn, reflecting their connection with this traditional form of knitting, in which cables symbolize ropes used by fishermen.

However, cables have a wonderfully versatile quality, and lend themselves equally well to fine silky yarns, crisp cottons and soft mohair yarns.

ribbed cable

worked over 7 sts

Rows 1, 3 and 5 (RS) K1 tbl, (P1 tbl, K1 tbl) 3 times.

Row 2 and every alternate row P1 tbl, (K1 tbl, P1 tbl) 3 times.

Row 7 Sl next 4 sts onto cable needle and hold at front of work, K1 tbl, P1, K1 tbl, sl 4th st from cable needle back onto LH needle and P1, then (K1 tbl, P1, K1 tbl) from cable needle.

Rows 9, 11, 13 and 15 as Row 1.

Row 16 as Row 2.

link cable

worked over 12 sts

Rows 1, 3 and 5 (RS) K12.
Rows 2, 4 and 6 P12.
Row 7 C6B, C6F.
Row 8 as Row 2.

deer cable

worked over 16 sts
Row 1 and every alternate row (WS) P16.
Row 2 K4, C4B, C4F, K4.
Row 4 K2, C4B, K4, C4F, K2.
Row 6 C4B, K8, C4F.

gull cable

worked over 7 sts

Row 1 RS K7.

Row 2 P7.

Row 3 Sl 2 sts onto cable needle and hold at back of work, K1 then K2 from cable needle, K1, sl 1 st onto cable needle and hold at front of work, K2 then K1 from cable needle.

Row 4 P7.

trellis cables

multiple of 6 plus 2 extra

Note 'C3B': sl next 2 sts onto cable needle and hold at back of work, K1, P2 from cable needle.

'C3F': sl next st onto cable needle and hold at front of work, P2, K1 from cable needle.

Rows 1 and 3 (RS) P3, *K2, P4, rep from * to last 5 sts, K2, P3.

Rows 2 and 4 K3, *P2, K4, rep from * to last 5 sts, P2, K3.

Row 5 P1, *C3B, C3F, rep from * to last st, P1.

Rows 6, 8 and 10 K1, P1, *K4, P2, rep from * to last 6 sts, K4, P1, K1.

Rows 7 and 9 P1, K1, *P4, K2, rep from * to last 6 sts, P4, K1, P1.

Row 11 P1, *C3F, C3B, rep from * to last st, P1.

Row 12 as Row 2.

interlaced cable

worked over 13 sts

Note 'Cr3F': sl next 2 sts onto cable needle and hold at front of work, P1, then K2 from cable needle.

'Cr3B': sl next st onto cable needle and hold at back of work, K2, then P1 from cable needle.

Row 1 (WS) P2, K2, P2, K1, P2, K2, P2.

Row 2 K2, P2, sl next 3 sts onto cable needle and hold at back of work, K2, sl P st from cable needle back onto LH needle and P it, K2 from cable needle, P2, K2.

Row 3 as Row 1.

Row 4 Cr3F, Cr3B, P1, Cr3F, Cr3B.

Row 5 K1, P4, K3, P4, K1.

Row 6 P1, C4B, P3, C4F, P1.

Row 7 as Row 5.

Row 8 Cr3B, Cr3F, P1, Cr3B, Cr3F.

Row 9 as Row 1.

Row 10 K2, P2, sl next 3 sts onto cable needle and hold at front of work, K2, sl P st from cable needle back onto LH needle and P it, K2 from cable needle, P2, K2.

Rows 11–16 as Rows 3–8.

special textures

bobble patterns

Bobbles are most attractive when they are combined with other elements, such as cables, eyelets and ribs. The half diamond cable with bobbles makes a striking vertical motif on a plain background – as does the nosegay pattern.

eyelet and bobble pattern

multiple of 9 plus 4 extra

Row 1 (RS) K1, *(yf, sl 1, K1, psso) twice, K5, rep from * to last 3 sts, K3.

Row 2 and every alternate row P.

Row 3 K2, *(yf, sl 1, K1, psso) twice, K5, rep from * to last 2 sts, K2.

Row 5 K3, *(yf, sl 1, K1, psso) twice, K5, rep from * to last st, K1.

Row 7 K4, *(yf, sl 1, K1, psso) twice, K2, **K into front and back of st twice, turn, P4, turn, K4, pass 2nd, 3rd and 4th sts over first st **, K2, rep from *.

Row 9 K3, *(K2 tog, yf) twice, K5, rep from * to last st, K1.

Row 11 K2, *(K2 tog, yf) twice, K5, rep from * to last 2 sts, K2.

Row 13 K1, *(K2 tog, yf) twice, K5, rep from * to last 3 sts, K3.

Row 15 *(K2 tog, yf) twice, K2, work from ** to ** of Row 7, K2, rep from * to last 4 sts, K4.

Row 16 P.

half diamond cable with bobbles

worked over 19 sts

Note 'C5B': sl 3 sts onto cable needle and hold at back of work, K2, put P st onto LH needle and P it, K2 from cable needle.
'Cr3B': see page 118.
'Cr3F': see page 118.

Rows 1 and 3 (WS) K7, P2, K1, P2, K7.

Row 2 P7, C5B, P7.

Row 4 P6, Cr3B, P1, Cr3F, P6.

Row 5 and every alternate row K all the K sts and P all the P sts.

Row 6 P5, Cr3B, P1, *(K1, P1, K1, P1, K1, P1, Kl) into next st, lift 2nd st on RH needle over first then separately lift the 3rd, 4th, 5th, 6th and 7th sts over the first st*, P1, Cr3F, P5.

Row 8 P4, Cr3B, (P1, work from * to * of Row 6) twice, P1, Cr3F, P4.

Row 10 P3, Cr3B, (P1, work from * to * of Row 6) three times, P1, Cr3F, P3.

Row 12 P2, Cr3B, P2, K2, P1, K2, P2, Cr3F, P2.

Row 14 P1, Cr3B, P3, K2, P1, K2, P3, Cr3F, P1.

simple bobble stitch

multiple of 6 plus 1 extra

Row 1 (RS) *K3, **K into front, back and front of next st, turn and K the 3 sts, turn and P the 3 sts, turn and K the 3 sts, turn and pass the 2nd st over the first st, pass the 3rd st over the first st, slip st onto RH needle, **, K2, rep from * to last st, K1.

Rows 2, 4 and 6 P.

Rows 3 and 5 K.

Row 7 *Work from ** to ** of Row 1, K5, rep from * to last st, work from ** to **.

Rows 8 and 10 P.

Rows 9 and 11 K.

Row 12 P.

nosegay pattern

worked over 16 sts

Note 'Cr2B': sl next st onto cable needle and hold at back of work, K1, then P1 from cable needle. 'Cr2F': sl next st onto cable needle and hold at front of work, P1, then K1 from cable needle. 'Make bobble': (K1, yf, K1, yf, K1) into next st, turn, P5, turn, K5, turn, P2 tog, P1, P2 tog, turn, sl 1, K2 tog, psso.

Row 1 (WS) K7, P2, K7.

Row 2 P6, C2B, C2F, P6.

Row 3 K5, Cr2F, P2, Cr2B, K5.

Row 4 P4, Cr2B, C2B, C2F, Cr2F, P4.

Row 5 K3, Cr2F, K1, P4, K1, Cr2B, K3.

Row 6 P2, Cr2B, P1, Cr2B, K2, Cr2F, P1, Cr2F, P2.

Row 7 (K2 P1) twice, K1, P2, K1, (P1, K2) twice.

Row 8 P2, make bobble, P1, Cr2B, P1, K2, P1, Cr2F, P1, make bobble, P2.

Row 9 K4, P1, K2, P2, K2, P1, K4.

Row 10 P4, make bobble, P2, K2, P2, make bobble, P4.

special textures

pattern potpourri

This collection of patterns includes the techniques of twisting and elongating stitches and grouping them together to create smocked effects. When practising these stitches, use a fairly stretchy yarn – a pure wool double knitting or four-ply is ideal. When you can work them smoothly, try them in some different yarns to discover their possibilities. Try smocked rib pattern, for example, in a glossy mercerized cotton, or elongated cross stitch in a glitter yarn.

alternating 2 x 2 rib

multiple of 4 plus 2 extra

Note 'Tw2L': K 2nd st tbl, K first st tbl, sl both sts off LH needle.

Rows 1 and 3 (RS) *K2, P2, rep from * to last 2 sts, K2.

Rows 2 and 4 *P2, K2, rep from * to last 2 sts, P2.

Row 5 *Tw2L, P2, rep from * to last 2 sts, Tw2L.

Rows 6 and 8 *K2, P2, rep from * to last 2 sts, K2.

Rows 7 and 9 *P2, K2, rep from * to last 2 sts, P2.

Row 10 *K2, P2, rep from * to last 2 sts, K2.

Row 11 *P2, Tw2L, rep from * to last 2 sts, P2.

Row 12 *P2, K2, rep from * to last 2 sts, P2.

crossed-stitch rib

multiple of 3 plus 1 extra
Note 'Tw2R': K into front of 2nd
st, K into front of first st, sl both
sts off LH needle.
Row 1 (RS) P1, *Tw2R, P1, rep
from *.
Row 2 K1,*P2, K1, rep from *.

linked check pattern

multiple of 10

Note 'Tw2R': K into front of 2nd st, then K into front of first st, sl both sts off LH needle.

'Tw2PL': P into 2nd st, sl this st over first st and off needle, P first st tbl. (This technique varies from the Tw2PL shown on page 100.)

Row 1 (RS) *K4, P2, Tw2R, P2, rep from *.

Row 2 *K2, Tw2PL, K2, P4, rep from *.

Rows 3 and 5 as Row 1.

Rows 4 and 6 as Row 2.

Row 7 *P1, Tw2R, P2, K4, P1, rep from *.

Row 8 *K1, P4, K2, Tw2PL, K1, rep from *.

Rows 9 and 11 as Row 7.

Rows 10 and 12 as Row 8.

tassel stitch

multiple of 6 plus 1 extra

Row 1 (RS) *K4, P2, rep from * to last st, K1.

Row 2 P1, *K2, P4, rep from *.

Row 3 as Row 1.

Row 4 as Row 2.

Row 5 *Put RH needle between 4th and 5th sts and draw through a loop, K1, P2, K3, rep from * to last st, K1.

Row 6 P1, *P3, K2, P2 tog, rep from *.

Row 7 K1, *P2, K4, rep from *.

Row 8 *P4, K2, rep from * to last st, P1.

Row 9 as Row 7.

Row 10 as Row 8.

Row 11 K3, *put RH needle between 4th and 5th sts and draw through a loop, K1, P2, K3, rep from * to last 4 sts, K1, P2, K1.

Row 12 P1, K2, P1, *P3, K2, P2 tog, rep from * to last 3 sts, P3.

elongated cross stitch

worked over any number of stitches
Work in rows of st st, g st or rev st
st to position for cross st.
Next row (RS) *Insert needle kw
into next st, take yarn under and
over RH needle, under and over
LH needle, and again under RH
needle. Draw loop through and
sl st off LH needle, rep from *.
Next row K or P into each st
according to patt.

smocked rib pattern

multiple of 16 plus 12 extra

Row 1 (RS) K3, P6, *K2, P2, K2, P2, K2, P6, rep from * to last 3 sts, K3.

Row 2 and every alternate row K the K sts and P the P sts as they appear.

Rows 3, 5 and 7 as Row 1.

Row 9 K3, *P2, K2, P2, **sl next 10 sts onto a cable needle, wind yarn anti-clockwise around needle 3 times, and on these 10 sts work K2, P6, K2**, rep from * to last 9 sts, P2, K2, P2, K3.

Row 10 P3, K2, P2, K2, P2, K6, P2, K2, P2, K2, P3.

Rows 11, 13, 15 and 17 K3, P2, K2, *P2, K2, P6, K2, P2, K2, rep from * to last 5 sts, P2, K3.

Row 19 K1, *work from ** to ** of Row 9, P2, K2, P2, rep from * to last 11 sts, work from ** to ** of Row 9, K1.

Row 20 as Row 2.

knitting in the round

Up to this point we have been concentrating on knitting back and forth in rows to produce flat pieces of fabric, which are then usually joined to make a garment. In this section we shall look at the technique of knitting in rounds to produce a seamless fabric – either tubular or flat. Tubular fabrics are used in many ways: for polo necks; for socks, gloves and hats; and sometimes for the main body of sweater. Flat medallion shapes can be sewn together to make a bedspread, for example; a large medallion can make a cushion cover or a shawl.

working in rounds

Knitting in rounds has several advantages over knitting in rows. For one thing, the right side of the work is always facing you, which means that certain stitch patterns are easier to form; for example, stocking/stockinette stitch is produced by knitting every row. Also, the fabric produced is seamless, which reduces the work involved in making up. Stitch patterns can be worked using only the repeat; without any edge stitches.

Two different kinds of needles are used for knitting in rounds: sets of double-pointed needles and circular needles. In some cases they are interchangeable; in others they are not. Whichever type you are using, there are several points to remember. First of all, it is important to keep track of the beginning of each round. To do this, place a ring marker or a loop of contrasting yarn at the beginning of the round, and slip it onto the right-hand needle as you begin each new round. It may also be necessary to mark certain shaping points or pattern repeats.

It is also important to work the first stitch of the round – and the first stitch on a new double-pointed needle – very firmly, in order to avoid producing a ladder effect at this point in the work.

When stitches are to be picked up for working in the round – at a neckline, for example – the pattern will specify the correct number for the stitch pattern repeat. However, if you are altering a pattern in which this section is knitted flat, you may need to adjust the number of stitches to make sure you have an exact multiple of the repeat. For example, if you are working a K2, P2 rib, the total number of stitches must be divisible by 4; otherwise, the stitch pattern will not join up correctly.

using a circular needle

Of the two kinds of needle used for knitting in the round, the circular needle is the easier to use. Only two needle points are involved in the work, and the bulk of the knitting slides easily between them as the work progresses. Also, there is only one join – as opposed to three or more if you are using double-pointed needles – so that it is easier to produce a smooth fabric. However, the circular needle cannot be used for small items, for the knitting must be able to reach from one point to the other without stretching.

Before beginning to work with a new circular needle or one that has been coiled up in the package for some time, straighten it by soaking it in warm water for about 15 minutes then pulling it gently through your fingers.

Many different patterns can
easily be achieved when knitting
in the round. Instructions for
knitting this circular target
medallion are given on page 156.

tubular knitting on a circular needle

1 Cast on the required number of stitches. If you are using a single-needle method of casting on, wind an elastic band around one end to prevent the stitches from slipping off. Before beginning to knit, make sure that the stitches reach easily from one point to the other. Hold the needle so that the end holding the last cast-on stitch is in your right hand and the one with the first cast-on stitch is in your left. Make sure that the stitches are not twisted on the needle; their lower edges should lie towards the centre of the ring. Place a ring marker or a loop of contrasting yarn over the RH point. Insert the point into the first stitch on the LH needle.

2 Work the first stitch, pulling the yarn firmly to prevent a gap at the join.

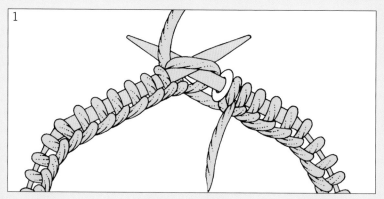

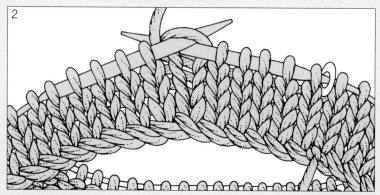

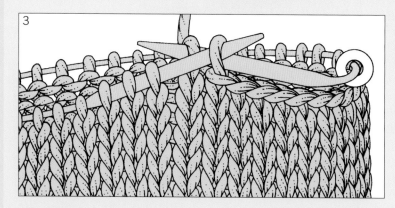

3 Work the first (right-side) round of the specified pattern around to the marker. Slip the marker and continue with the second round of the pattern. Continue working in the chosen pattern (see page 151) as set. Cast/bind off in the usual way. After drawing the thread through the last stitch, take it through the first stitch of the round.

working in rows with a circular needle

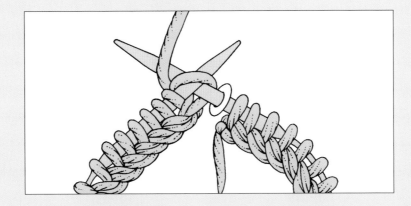

A circular needle is useful for working in rows. The weight of the work is distributed equally along the needle, which is ideal for large, heavy pieces, which can be tiring to work on a pair of ordinary needles. Substituting a circular needle is also a good idea when knitting on a train journey, for example, when ordinary needles may be awkward. To use a circular needle in this way, cast on in the chosen method. Work the first row beginning with the last cast-on stitch, rather than the first one, as in tubular knitting. At the end of the row, turn the needle so that the point with the last-worked stitch is in your left hand, and work the next row.

double-pointed needles

Double-pointed needles are often used to pick up stitches around a neckline, in which case the technique is basically the same as shown on page 65. The total number of stitches may be divided evenly among the three or four needles; or the division may be based on the shape of the work: a V neck, for example, might be divided into right front, left front and back, with a needle for each.

For small items double-pointed needles are used from the outset of the work. In traditional Guernsey and Fair Isle knitting, sets of extra-long double-pointed needles are used to knit virtually the entire garment.

tubular fabric on double-pointed needles

1 Begin by casting the required number of stitches onto a single-pointed needle of the same size as the double-pointed needles (or a larger size, if a loose edge is desired). The illustrations show the stitches as cast on by the thumb method, but any method could be used. Slip the stitches onto the double-pointed needles, leaving one needle free for working the stitches. Here, three needles out of a set of four are used.

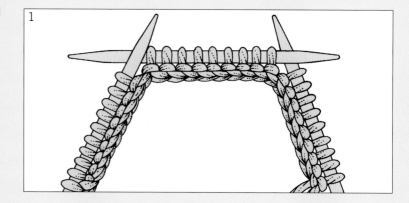

tip

When resuming work on a piece of knitting worked on double-pointed needles, undo two or three stitches and work them again. They will have stretched slightly, and the interruption might (depending on the stitch pattern) be quite noticeable. The same applies to knitting worked in rows on ordinary needles, if you have had to stop in the middle of a row.

2 Arrange the needles so that their points cross as shown. Check to make sure that the stitches are not twisted. Place a ring marker over the point holding the last cast-on stitch. With the remaining needle, knit the first cast-on stitch; draw the yarn firmly to close the gap.

3 Continue working into all the stitches on the first needle. When this needle is free, use it to work into the stitches on the second needle. Continue in this way, taking care to pull the yarn firmly when working the first stitch on the new needle and slipping the marker at the beginning of each new round. When the work is the required depth, cast/bind off as usual. Draw the yarn through the first stitch of the round to make a neat join.

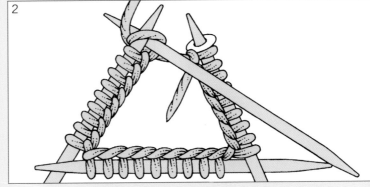

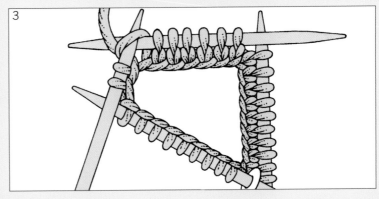

medallions

By working in rounds and increasing in a regular sequence it is possible to make a variety of medallion shapes. Medallions have a number of different uses. A single medallion can be used as the back of a baby's bonnet or the top of a beret. If extended, it can become a shawl. Individual medallions can be sewn or crocheted together to make a tablecloth or bedspread.

Medallions are normally worked from the centre outwards, although it is also possible to work them from the outer edge inwards, by means of decreasing rather than increasing.

If the increases are worked at the same point on every round, they will form a pattern of straight lines radiating outwards from the centre. If they are moved, a swirl pattern is produced.

The type of increase worked will also affect the appearance of the medallions. Bar increases (see page 56) will produce an embossed effect, raised increases a more subtle pattern. For a more decorative effect, an openwork increase is used.

Medallions must be worked on double-pointed needles (although a circular needle can be substituted on the outer rounds of a shawl). The number of needles used varies with the shape and with personal preference. A square medallion is best worked on four, knitting with a fifth; a pentagon, on five; a hexagon, on three (two sections per needle).

It must be admitted that medallion knitting is not simple. However, once you are past the first few rounds it becomes much easier. For your initial practice, use a moderately stretchy, smooth yarn in a light to medium colour.

crocheted foundation

You may find this method of beginning a medallion easier than the cast-on method, especially where there are only 8 stitches in the first round.

Crochet a chain (see page 204) consisting of 8 stitches, including the slip loop. Join the first and last chain with a slip stitch. Using 4 double-pointed needles, pick up 1 stitch for each chain. Insert the needle through the top of the chain as shown.

working a square medallion

Cast 8 stitches onto a double-pointed needle using the cable method (see page 19). Or you may prefer to use the French two-needle cast-on. This is like the cable method, but the needle is inserted into the stitches themselves, rather than between them.

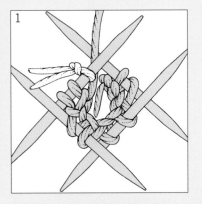

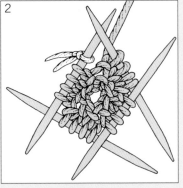

1 Arrange the stitches on 4 needles, as shown, and tie a thread marker at the beginning of the round – just before the last cast-on stitch.

2 (Round 1) Using the fifth needle, knit into the back of every stitch. (Round 2) Knit into the front and back of every stitch: 16 stitches on the needles.

3 (Round 3) Knit every stitch in the normal way. (Round 4) Knit into the front and back of the first stitch, knit 1, knit into the front and back of the third stitch, knit 1. Placing the bar 1 stitch in from the corner makes the line of increasing symmetrical. Repeat on the remaining 3 sets of 4 stitches: 24 stitches. Repeat rounds 3 and 4 until the medallion is the desired size. Cast/bind off.

shaping a gusset

A traditional Guernsey sweater is knitted mainly in the round. Even the sleeves are worked in this way, on stitches picked up from the yoke. The shaping incorporates an underarm gusset, which helps to make the garment comfortable.

Although a gusset can be worked separately and sewn in, it is not difficult to knit one in as shown here, while working in the round.

The garment is worked in the round up to the armpit. To indicate the side 'seams', purl a single stitch at these points on each round. At the widest part of the gusset the tubular knitting is interrupted and the front and back completed separately working in rows. Then stitches are picked up for the sleeves and the tubular knitting recommenced. The gusset stitches are decreased down to a single purled stitch for the sleeve 'seam'.

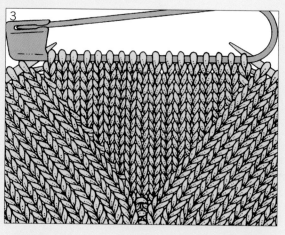

1 To begin shaping the gusset, increase 1 stitch on either side of the 'seam' by working a 'make 1' increase (see page 56) just before the purled stitch, knitting the stitch, then increasing again just after it.

2 On the next round, purl across all stitches.

3 On the next round, work up to the 3 gusset stitches, make 1, work across gusset, make 1. Continue in this way, adding 2 stitches to the gusset on alternate rounds, until it is the desired width. Work one round straight; slip the gusset stitches onto a stitch holder.

4 Complete the front and back sections separately. Join the shoulder seams.

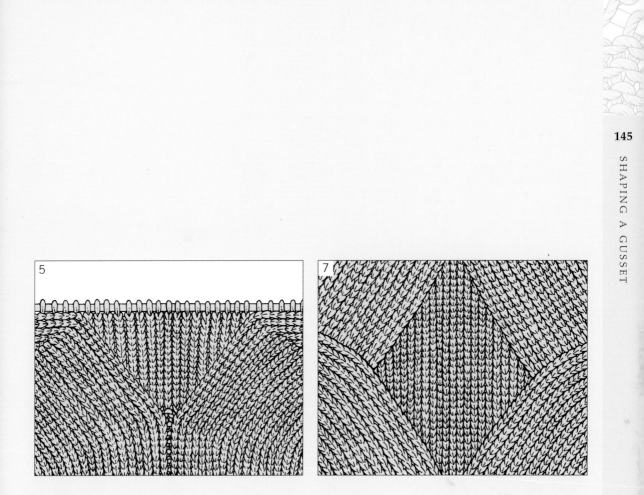

5 Using a set of double-pointed needles, knit across the gusset stitches, then pick up and knit the stitches for the sleeve from the front and back of the garment.

6 Work the sleeve downwards, decreasing on either side of the gusset. On the first round: Sl 1, K1, psso, K to last 2 gusset sts, K2 tog. Work the next round without decreasing.

7 Continue to decrease 2 stitches on alternate rounds until 1 stitch remains in the gusset. This marks the sleeve 'seam'; purl it on every round.

turning a heel

Socks are nearly always worked in the round, on double-pointed needles, in order to avoid the discomfort of a seam. The only complicated shaping involved is turning the heel, but even this is less difficult than it appears at first glance.

There are several basic methods of turning a heel; the one shown in these illustrations is called a Dutch heel. The shaping involves a technique known as short-row shaping, in which some stitches are merely held on the needle while others are worked. In turning a heel the held stitches are gradually decreased and incorporated into the centre section of the heel, then the heel is rejoined to the instep stitches.

The main part of a sock is normally worked in stocking/stockinette stitch, because it is smooth and comfortable. Single ribbing is the usual choice for the upper edge of the sock because it grips the ankle neatly. Take care to cast on loosely so that the edge will not be uncomfortably tight.

1 Using a set of 4 double-pointed needles, cast on the specified number of stitches for the sock. The number should be divisible by 3 and also – if you are working in K1, P1 rib – by 2. Here the number is 42. Work in single rib (or other rib pattern) for the required length down to the top of the heel. Fasten off.

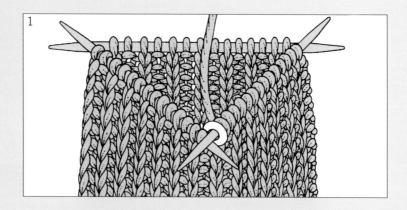

2 Now divide the heel stitches from those that will be used for the instep. The respective numbers will vary according to the pattern and the size; here, 22 stitches are used for the heel. Slip the first 11 stitches of the round and the last 11 onto one double-pointed needle. Slip the remaining instep stitches onto a spare needle; a short circular needle is convenient for this, as it holds the stitches in a curve, out of the way.

3 Rejoin the yarn to the RH edge of the heel stitches. Work in rows, in stocking/stockinette stitch, until the heel is the required depth from ankle to bottom of heel, ending with a purl

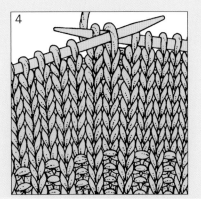

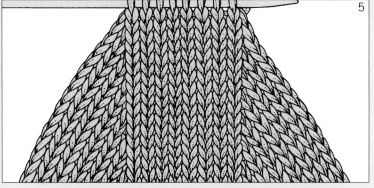

4 On the next row, work across the first 14 stitches (the number will vary with the pattern, but should be approximately two thirds of the total), then decrease 1 stitch as follows: sl 1, K1, psso. Turn, leaving the remaining stitches unworked. There are 15 stitches on the needle.

5 Purl across the first 7 stitches, then decrease 1 stitch: P2 tog. Turn, leaving the remaining stitches unworked. Continue working on the centre stitches; at the end of every row work in 1 of the held stitches, at the same time decreasing 1 stitch. On knit rows decrease as in step 5; on purl rows, decrease as in step 6. Continue in this way until there are 8 stitches on the needle (that is, when all the held stitches have been decreased), ending with a wrong-side row.

6 Resume working in rounds on the 3 double-pointed needles. Work across the heel stitches, then pick up and knit the specified number along the left side of the heel; here it is 10 stitches. Using a second needle, work across the instep stitches. Using a third needle, pick up 10 stitches (or the specified number) along the right side of the heel, then knit across half of the heel stitches. Place a marker at this point to indicate the beginning of the round. At this point there are 48 stitches on the needles.

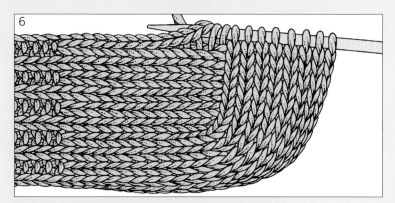

7 Work one round straight. Begin to decrease the stitches to either side of the instep: work to the last 3 stitches on the first needle, K2 tog, work across the instep stitches, work the first stitch on third needle, then sl 1, K1, psso, work to the end.

8 Repeat this decrease round until the specified number of stitches remain on the needles. The sock is then worked straight until the toe shaping.

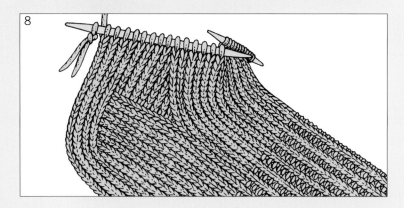

joining in new yarn

It should not be necessary to join yarn in mid-row when working in rows, if you re-wind the yarn; however, this cannot be avoided in circular knitting. If the fabric is smooth, it is important to place the join at an inconspicuous place on the garment; on a textured fabric it may be possible to join yarn almost anywhere within the round. Either of the following two method can be used, depending on the yarn and the stitch pattern.

threading-in method

This method of joining yarn is preferred when working stocking/stockinette stitch in a smooth yarn.

Thread the end of the new yarn into a tapestry needle. Take it through the old yarn for about 4 cm (1½ in). Continue knitting, working in the joined yarn. Trim the loose ends later.

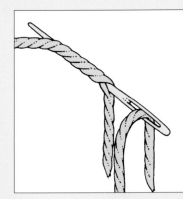

double strand method

This method can be used if the yarn is fuzzy and the stitch pattern a textured one. The first stitch in the new yarn should be a knit stitch.

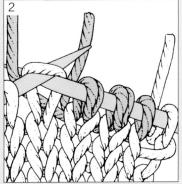

1 Having worked the last stitch in the old yarn, let this yarn drop down on the wrong side of the work. Turn back the end of the new yarn for 10 cm (4 in). Insert the needle into the next stitch and draw through the loop of the new yarn, so forming the first stitch in the new yarn.

2 Work the next two or three stitches in the double strand, then let the short end drop. On the following round, treat these double strands as one. Trim the short end of new yarn close to the work. Darn the old yarn into the wrong side (see page 73).

stitch patterns in rounds

Instructions for stitch patterns are normally given for working in rows. The knitter wishing to work in the round may therefore be put off the idea, thinking that they will be able to use only the basic stitches.

Happily, there are many stitch patterns that can easily be converted for working in the round. As already noted (see page 136), stocking/stockinette stitch is produced by knitting every round. Conversely, reverse stocking/stockinette stitch results if every round is purled. For garter stitch, you knit and purl alternate rounds. For most rib patterns, you simply knit and purl the same stitches on every round. The principle, therefore, is that any stitch normally purled on a wrong-side row will be knitted when worked on the right side, and vice versa.

Any stitch pattern in which every wrong-side row is simply purled can easily be worked in the round by knitting all these rows.

If you wish to use a more complex stitch pattern, you may need first to work a sample in rows, until you become familiar with its construction. Then write your own revised instructions and work a sample in the round. Remember, when working in the round, to omit the edge stitches.

The patterns below and on the right are some of the stitch patterns given elsewhere in the book, with instructions converted for working in the round.

irish moss/seed stitch (see page 34)
multiple of 2
Rounds 1 and 2 *K1, P1, rep from *.
Rounds 3 and 4 *P1, K1, rep from *.

diamond seed (see page 35)
multiple of 8
Round 1 *P1, K7, rep from *.
Rounds 2 and 8 *K1, P1, K5, P1, rep from *.
Rounds 3 and 7 *K2, P1, K3, P1, K1, rep from *.
Rounds 4 and 6 *K3, P1, K1, P1, K2, rep from *.
Round 5 *K4, P1, K3, rep from *.

The instructions for making these effective stitch patterns have been adapted for working in the round. From left to right: Irish Moss/Seed; Diamond Seed; Embossed Chevron; Nut Pattern.

embossed chevron (see page 41)
multiple of 12
Rounds 1 and 2 *K3, P5, K3, P1, rep from *.
Rounds 3 and 4 *P1, K3, P2, rep from *.
Rounds 5 and 6 *P2, K3, P1, K3, P3, rep from *.
Rounds 7 and 8 *P3, K5, P3, K1, rep from *.
Rounds 9 and 10 *K1, P3, K3, P3, K2, rep from *.
Rounds 11 and 12 *K2, P3, K1, P3, K3, rep from *.

nut pattern (see page 76)
multiple of 4
Round 1 *P3, (K1, yf, K1) into next st, rep from *.
Rounds 2 and 3 *P3, K3, rep from *.
Round 4 *P3, K3tog, rep from *.
Rounds 5 and 6 P.
Round 7 *P1, (K1, yf, K1) into next st, P2, rep from *.
Rounds 8 and 9 *P1, K3, P2, rep from *.
Round 10 *P1, K3tog, P2, rep from *.
Rounds 11 and 12 P.

medallion patterns

These four medallions include the basic shapes and the different methods of placing and working increases. They have been worked here in a crisp double-knitting-weight mercerized cotton, which shows off their method of construction.

Once you have become adept at the method of working medallions you will find that they offer a huge variety of creative possibilities. You can introduce stripes and other colour patterns. Or you can work the medallion in a stitch pattern – although it is best to work this out on paper first, at least for the first few rounds to be worked in the pattern. Once the pattern is established, you should be able to bring the increased stitches into the pattern with no more difficulty than in shaping a piece of row-by-row flat knitting.

For the basic technique of working a medallion, see page 142.

maltese cross medallion

Cast on 8 sts. (In this example, a crocheted chain [see page 204] has been used as the foundation.) Arrange the sts evenly on 4 needles, and use a fifth for the knitting.

Round 1 K every st tbl.

Round 2 *K1, yf, rep from *: 16 sts.

Round 3 and every alternate round K.

Round 4 K1, *yf, K2, rep from * to last st, yf, K1: 24 sts.

Round 6 K2, *yf, K2, yf, K4, rep from * ending last rep K2 instead of K4: 32 sts.

Cont in this way, inc to either side of the 2 centre sts on each needle on alternate rounds, until the medallion is the required size. Cast/bind off loosely.

For a solid medallion work as above, but work a bar inc or a 'make 1' inc to either side of the centre 2 sts.

swirl hexagon

Cast on 12 sts. (A knitted foundation has been used for this example.) Divide the sts evenly onto 3 needles, and K with a fourth.

Round 1 K every st tbl.

Round 2 *Yf, K2, rep from *: 18 sts.

Round 3 and every alternate round K.

Round 4 *Yf, K3, rep from *: 24 sts.

Round 6 *'Yf, K4, rep from *: 30 sts.

Cont in this way until hexagon is the required size.

Cast/bind off loosely.

circular target medallion

Cast on 8 sts. (In this example, a crocheted chain [see page 204] has been used as the foundation.) Arrange the sts evenly on 4 needles, and use a fifth for the knitting.

Round 1 K every st tbl.

Round 2 *Yf, K1, rep from *: 16 sts.

Rounds 3, 4 and 5 K.

Round 6 *Yf, K1, rep from *: 32 sts.

Rounds 7–11 K.

Round 12 *Yf, K1, rep from *: 64 sts.

Rounds 13–19 K.

The example shown has been worked up to Round 14, then cast/bind off and finished with a crocheted edging. To make the medallion larger, cont as follows:

Round 20 *Yf, K2, rep from *: 96 sts.

Rounds 21–25 K.

Round 26 *Yf, K3, rep from *: 128 sts.

Rounds 25–31 K.

Round 32 *Yf, K4, rep from *: 160 sts.

Cont in this way, working 5 plain rounds between every inc round and inc 32 sts on every subsequent inc round, spacing them evenly (so that, for example Round 38 will have 5 K sts between the inc).

pentagon

Cast on 10 sts. (In this example, a knitted foundation has been used.) Divide the sts onto 3 needles as follows:
needle 1, 2 sts;
needle 2, 4 sts;
needle 3, 4 sts.
Beg by working on these 3 needles, knitting with a fourth; when the work becomes large enough to accommodate more needles, divide the sts evenly onto 5 needles and K with a sixth.
Round 1 K every st tbl.
Round 2 *K1, M1, rep from *: 20 sts.
Round 3 K.
Round 4 *K1, M1, K3, M1, rep from *: 30 sts.
Round 5 K.
Round 6 K.
Round 7 *K1, M1, K5, M1, rep from *: 40 sts.
Round 8 K.
Round 9 *K1, M1, K7, M1, rep from *: 50 sts.
Cont to work in this way, inc to either side of the st at the beg of each section and working 2 plain rounds and 1 plain round

alternately between the inc rounds. Cast/bind off loosely when the medallion is the required size.

For an openwork effect work a 'yarn forward' inc instead of a 'make 1' inc.

colourwork

There are many ways of combining two or more colours in a piece of knitting – some complex, some extremely simple, all capable of producing rich and exciting effects. They include simple horizontal stripes, fascinating slipstitch patterns – some with interesting textures as well, jacquard motifs and traditional Fair Isle designs.

Many commercially produced patterns include colourwork; but it is also possible to add a colour pattern to a one-colour design, thereby giving it a stamp of individuality.

horizontal stripes

An infinite number of effects can be created simply by working rows in different colours to produce horizontal stripes. The simplest version is a two-colour stripe, with the colours changed after a regular number of rows. Worked in stocking/stockinette stitch, this has a neat, crisp appearance. More subtle effects can be achieved by using several shades of the same colour; by varying the number of rows worked, in a regular or random pattern; by using the purled side of the work, so that the colour changes have a broken appearance; or by introducing the occasional purled row on the right side of a stocking/stockinette stitch fabric for textural interest.

Horizontal stripes need not run horizontally. If you work the garment from one side edge to other – a method often used for batwing pullovers and cardigans – the stripes will run vertically. (True vertical stripes are produced by using one of the methods shown on pages 164–165.) Zigzag stripes will result if you work horizontal stripes in a chevron stitch pattern.

Discover the fun of creating your own striped patterns by working samples in leftover yarns. Keep the samples for reference when designing.

joining new colours

1 Tie the new colour to the old one at the RH edge of the work, using a double knot. Do not cut off the old yarn.

2 Continue knitting with the new yarn. On every second row twist the two yarns around each other to help keep the edge neat. When changing back to the first colour, bring it in front of the second colour. Avoid pulling it tightly when beginning to knit with the new yarn.

If the yarn is fine, up to three colours can be carried up the side in this way. Where more colours are used, or where one colour is not used for many rows, they should be cut off and rejoined as required. This is also necessary, of course, where new colours are introduced on wrong-side rows and so joined at the LH edge.

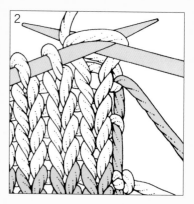

Horizontal stripes can be simply worked by changing colour at the side edge. Here the colours have been changed on every second row.

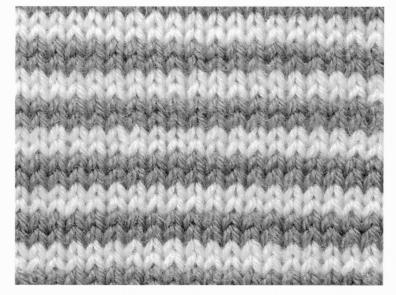

Chevron stripes have been created here by working the chevron stitch pattern given on page 81 and changing colour as for ordinary horizontal stripes.

slipstitch colour patterns

Also called mosaic patterns, slipstitch colour patterns can look difficult but are actually quite simple to work. Only one colour is used in a row; the blended colour effects are achieved by slipping some stitches, so that the colour from the previous row encroaches upon that of the row being worked. The working yarn is carried loosely behind the slipped stitches.

The fabric produced by most slipstitch colour patterns is a dense one. In some patterns the stitches draw in, so that more stitches are required for a given width. Thus it is important, if you are substituting a slipstitch pattern for another stitch, to make a good-sized tension/gauge swatch.

The stitches slipped in these patterns are always slipped purlwise, as shown in the example below. Note also that the instructions 'with yarn to front' and 'with yarn back' refer to the back and front in relation to the knitter; they do not mean the right and wrong sides of the work. The yarn is taken directly to the front or back and not taken over the needle. After slipping the stitch(es), you must then, of course, have the yarn at the back if the next stitch is a knit stitch or at the front if it is a purl stitch.

basic slipstitch technique

The simple pattern shown here – called tricolour wave stripe – will introduce you to the principles of working slipstitch colour patterns.

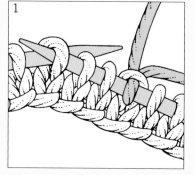 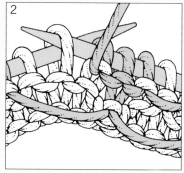

1 First cast on a multiple of 4 stitches plus 1, using colour A. P one row.
Row 1 (RS) With B, K1, * with yarn back sl 3 pw, K1, rep from * to end.

2 **Row 2** With B, P2, * with yarn to front sl 1, P3, rep from * to last 3 sts, sl 1, P2.
Row 3 With B, K to end.
Row 4 With B, P to end.
Rows 5–8 With C, rep Rows 1–4.
Rows 9–12 With A, rep Rows 1–4.

The right side of tricolour
wave stripe illustrates the
construction of a typical
slipstitch colour pattern.

The reverse side of tricolour
wave stripe demonstrates how
yarn is carried from one stitch
to another.

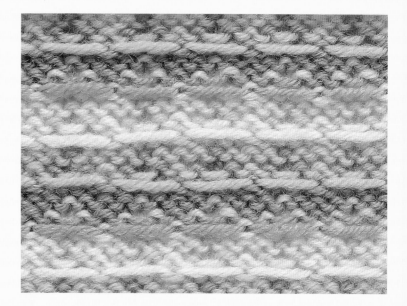

vertical colour changes

Colour patterns with more than one colour in a row are worked by one of several methods: carrying, or 'stranding', the unused colour loosely along the back of the work until it is needed again; 'weaving' the unused yarn into the work at intervals, or with every alternate stitch, until it is needed; and working with several different balls of yarn, positioned across the work and picked up as required – a method called 'intarsia'.

The choice of method is dictated by the type of design, but also by the weight and colour of the yarn. A repeating-motif pattern, such as a traditional Fair Isle design, that uses only two colours in any one row is normally knitted using the stranding method, with weaving incorporated where the unused yarn must span long distances.

A design that includes more than two colours in a row will usually be knitted by the intarsia method, because carrying more than two colours across every row would make the work too bulky. However, a two-colour vertical stripe pattern with, say, 10 stitches in each stripe would also be knitted using the intarsia method because the stranding method would leave long strands of yarn – likely to be snagged – on the wrong side, and weaving in the yarn might leave noticeable marks on the right side: weaving is better suited to 'busy' patterns. Care must also be taken, especially with fine yarns, that dark colours do not show through light ones on the right side. It is best to make a sample first to determine whether this is likely to be a problem.

intarsia method

Designs requiring the intarsia method include wide vertical or diagonal stripes, large repeating motifs, individual motifs and pictorial knitting.

The first step is to prepare the yarn by winding it onto bobbins. These do not unroll as balls of yarn do, and so are less likely to become tangled. It is possible to buy plastic bobbins at some yarn shops; however, if the yarn you are using is thick, you may prefer to make your own bobbins of the desired size from pieces of cardboard.

Motifs designed to be worked using the intarsia method can sometimes be more easily worked in Swiss darning (see page 206).

In the illustrations opposite the fabric being worked is stocking/stockinette stitch; in the case of reverse stocking/stockinette stitch the yarns are held on the knit side of the work. However, the process of twisting the yarns is essentially the same: the old yarn is taken over the new yarn, which is then brought up in the correct position for working.

changing colour on a knit row

Work in the first colour to the point for the colour change. If the second colour is being introduced for the first time, tie it to the first colour. On subsequent rows the procedure is as follows:

Drop the first colour *over* the second, pick up the second colour and continue knitting with it. In this way, the yarns are twisted around each other. If this were not done, the two areas of colour would be separate, leaving a split in the fabric.

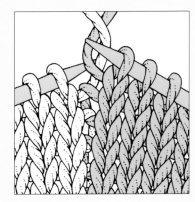

making a bobbin

Cut a cardboard rectangle of the desired size. For thick yarns, about 5 by 8 cm (2 by 3½ in) will do. In each short end, cut notches as shown. Wind the yarn through the notches.

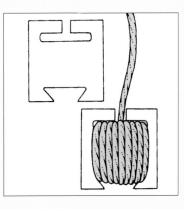

changing colour on a purl row

Work in the first colour to the point for the colour change. Drop the first colour over the second, pick up the second and continue purling with it. On both knit and purl rows, work the stitches before and after the change fairly tightly to avoid leaving a gap.

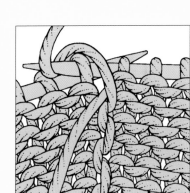

stranding yarns

Stranding is the basic technique used when knitting a repeating motif using two colours that are alternated at short intervals. As a general rule yarns should not be stranded across more than five stitches; otherwise the elasticity of the work is likely to be impaired. Where yarn must be carried for more than five stitches, it should be woven into the work, using the techniques shown on pages 168–169.

Both stranding and weaving are easier to do on knit rows than on purl rows, and when working in rounds (see page 136). Whether you work in rounds or in rows, however, it is most important to hold the unused yarn loosely in order to avoid puckering the fabric. For a smooth tension/gauge it is best to hold one yarn in each hand, so combining the right-hand and the left-hand methods (see pages 22–23). You will find the new method awkward at first, but it is worthwhile persevering with it if you plan to do much colour-patterned knitting.

stranding yarn on a knit row

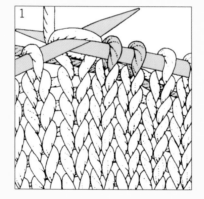

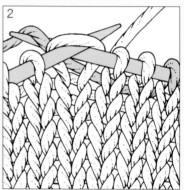

1 On the row in which the second colour is introduced, join it at the RH edge. Begin knitting in the colour specified by the pattern, carrying the other colour loosely across the back of the work. To knit with the RH yarn, hold the LH yarn slightly under the needles.

2 To knit with the LH yarn, hold the RH yarn out of the way.

stranding on a purl row

Here the process is the same as for a knit row except that the stranded yarn is held at the front of the work.

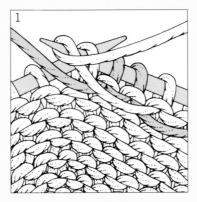

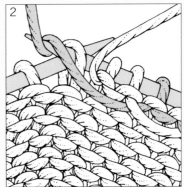

1 To purl with the RH yarn, hold the left under the needles.

2 To purl with the LH yarn, hold the right out of the way.

tip

To prevent a ball of yarn from rolling around while you are knitting, simply place it in a bowl or a jar on the floor. This is especially helpful when working with two yarns simultaneously – a bowl placed on either side of you will keep the yarns from becoming tangled.

The best way of working a Fair Isle pattern is to hold one colour in each hand, as shown, knitting with them alternately and stranding or weaving the unused colour into the back of the work.

weaving yarns

Before learning the weaving technique, it is advisable to master the stranding technique. In stranding the unused yarn is always kept out of the way of the yarn being worked. In weaving, the unused yarn is occasionally incorporated into a stitch. This can be done on every alternate stitch and produces a dense fabric with no loose strands on the wrong side. Or it can be done every few stitches. Avoid working the yarn into stitches directly above each other, as this may cause a visible indentation in the fabric.

Start by working in the round. Otherwise, cast 50 or more stitches onto a pair of needles and work in rows, breaking off one yarn at the end of each knit row, then purling back to the right-hand edge and rejoining the contrasting colour for the next row of weaving. When you can weave on a knit row, try weaving the yarns while purling.

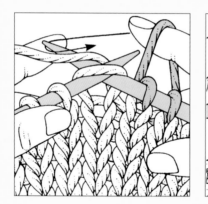

knitting – weaving in LH yarn

When knitting with the RH yarn, take the LH yarn alternately below and above the stitches.

To weave the LH yarn below, simply hold it under the work as if for stranding (see page 166).

To weave the LH yarn above, take it over the RH needle. Take the RH yarn around the needle to knit; draw this loop through the stitch.

purling – weaving in LH yarn

When purling with the RH yarn, take the LH yarn alternately below and above the stitches.

To weave the LH yarn below, simply hold it away from the work as if for stranding (see page 166).

To weave the LH yarn above, take it over the RH needle (but not all the way around it), and purl (left) with the RH yarn.

knitting – weaving in RH yarn

To weave the RH yarn above, simply hold it away from the work as if for stranding (see page 166) and knit with the LH yarn.

To take the RH yarn below:

1 Bring the RH yarn around the needle as if to knit.

2 Bring the LH yarn around the needle as if to knit.

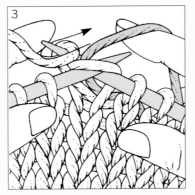

3 Reverse the RH yarn, taking it to the left and under the needle point – and thus off the needle.

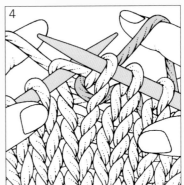

4 Complete the stitch in the LH yarn.

purling – weaving in RH yarn

To weave the RH yarn above, simply hold it away from the work as if for stranding (see page 166), and purl with the LH yarn.

To weave the RH yarn below:

1 Loop the RH yarn around the needle as shown.

2 Bring the LH yarn over the needle as if to purl.

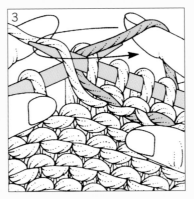

3 Reverse the RH yarn, taking it to the left and under the needle point – and thus off the needle.

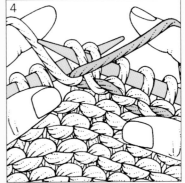

4 Complete the stitch in the LH yarn.

following a chart

Individual and repeating motifs for colour patterns are often given in the form of a chart, which is easier to follow than written row-by-row instructions. The colours themselves may be shown on the chart, or they may be represented by symbols, identified in an accompanying key. Each square on the chart represents a single stitch.

   The chart is worked from bottom to top. Right-side rows are normally given odd numbers; they are worked from right to left. The even-numbered, wrong-side rows are worked from left to right. This rule, however, does not apply to working in rounds (see page 136) in which all the rows are knitted from right to left.

   Charts for repeating motifs normally include only the one repeat, along with any edge stitches required. The repeat itself is marked off with a heavy line; where several sizes are given there may be additional edge stitches given for the larger sizes.

Two simple charts: one for an individual motif and one for a repeat pattern. In the duck motif only one contrasting colour is used, represented by a dot. For this simple motif only every fifth row is marked, plus the final 16th row.

Key

☐ A

◉ B

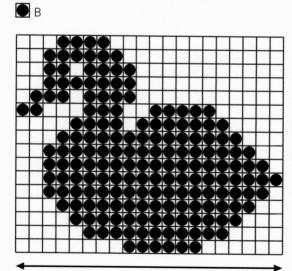

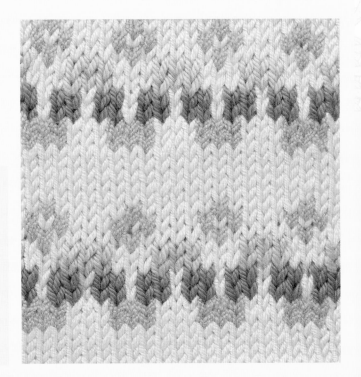

tip

When following a chart, it is important to keep careful track of your progress. A good way of doing this is to have the chart photocopied (several times, if it is to be repeated vertically) and draw a line through each row when it is completed. If the chart is small, having it enlarged by the photocopier will make it easier to follow.

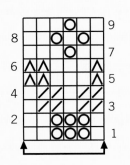

Key

☐	A
◙	B
▨	C
⏶	D

The slightly more complicated Fair Isle motif uses three contrasting colours, with every row marked.

slipstitch colourwork

Like most other forms of colourwork, slipstitch patterns have a marvellously versatile character. They can change beyond recognition if you play around with the choice of colours. Try substituting dark for light shades in some of these patterns.

The fabric produced by slipstitch patterns is quite dense, which makes them ideal for a jacket.

Remember that the stitches are slipped purlwise, unless otherwise stated.

three-colour tweed

multiple of 3 plus 1 extra
Note Colour A = yellow, Colour B = dark blue, Colour C = pale blue.
Row 1 (WS) With A, K.
Row 2 With B, K3, *sl 1 wyb, K2, rep from * to last st, K1.
Row 3 With B, K3, *sl 1 wyf, K2, rep from * to last st, K1.
Row 4 With C, *K2, sl 1 wyb, rep from * to last st, K1.
Row 5 With C, K1, *sl 1 wyf, K2, rep from *.
Row 6 With A, K1, *sl 1 wyb, K2, rep from *.
Row 7 With A, *K2, sl 1 wyf, rep from * to last st, K1.
Rep Rows 2 to 7.

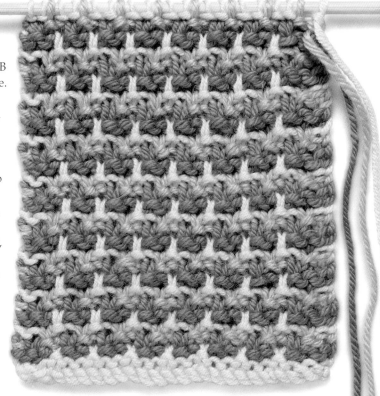

linked stripe pattern

multiple of 4

Note Colour A = yellow, Colour B = turquoise.

Rows 1 (RS), 2, 5 and 6 With A, K.

Rows 3 and 7 With B, K1, *sl 2 wyb, K2, rep from * ending sl 2, K1.

Rows 4 and 8 With B, P1, *sl 2 wyf, P2, rep from * ending sl 2, P1.

Rows 9, 10, 13 and 14 With B, K.

Rows 11 and 15 With A, K1, *sl 2 wyb, K2, rep from * ending sl 2, K1.

Rows 12 and 16 With A, P1, *sl 2 wyf, P2, rep from * ending sl 2, P1.

corn on the cob stitch

multiple of 2
Note Colour A = yellow, Colour B
= mauve.
Cast on with A and K one row.
Row 1 (RS) With B, K1, *K1,
sl 1 wyb, rep from *ending K1.
Row 2 With B, K1, * sl 1 wyf,
K1 tbl, rep from * ending K1.
Row 3 With A, K1, *sl 1 wyb,
K1 tbl, rep from * ending K1.
Row 4 With A, K1, *K1, sl 1 wyf,
rep from *ending K1.

shadow box pattern

multiple of 4 plus 3 extra

Note Colour A = yellow, Colour B = pink, Colour C = beige.

Row 1 (RS) With A, K.

Row 2 With A, K1, *K1 wrapping yarn twice around needle, K3, rep from * ending last rep K1.

Row 3 With B, K1, *sl 1 wyb dropping extra loop, K3, rep from * ending last rep K1.

Row 4 With B, K1, *sl 1 wyf, K3, rep from * ending last rep K1.

Row 5 With C, K1, *sl 2 wyb, K2, rep from * ending sl 1, K1.

Row 6 With C, K1, sl 1 wyf, *P2, sl 2 wyf, rep from * ending K1.

ladders

multiple of 6 plus 5 extra
Note Colour A = yellow, Colour B = green.

Row 1 (RS) With A, K2, *sl 1 wyb, K5, rep from * to last 3 sts, sl 1 wyb, K2.

Row 2 With A, P2, sl 1 wyf, *P5, sl 1 wyf, rep from * to last 2 sts, P2.

Row 3 With B, *K5, sl 1 wyb, rep from * to last 5 sts, K5.

Row 4 With B, *K5, sl 1 wyf, rep from * to last 5 sts, K5.

multicoloured stripes

multiple of 4 plus 3 extra

Note Colour A = yellow, Colour B = turquoise, Colour C = blue, Colour D = pink.

Row 1 (WS) With A, P.

Row 2 With B, K2, *sl 1 wyb, K1, rep from * to last st, K1,

Row 3 With B, P2, *sl 1 wyf, P1, rep from * to last st, P1.

Row 4 With C, K1, *sl 1 wyb, K1, rep from *.

Row 5 With C, P.

Row 6 With D. K1, *sl 1 wyb, K3, rep from * to last 2 sts, sl 1 wyb, K1.

Row 7 With D, P1, *sl 1 wyf, P3, rep from * to last 2 sts, sl 1 wyf, P1.

Row 8 With B, K2, *sl 3 wyb, K1, rep from * to last st, K1.

Row 9 With B, *P3, sl 1 wyf, rep from * to last 3 sts, P3.

Row 10 With A, K1, *sl 1 wyb, K3, rep from * to last 2 sts, sl 1 wyb, K1.

jacquard patterns

The term 'jacquard' is commonly applied to repeating colourwork motifs. (The word is derived from a loom producing figured fabrics invented in the 18th century by Joseph Jacquard.) Depending on the scale and complexity of the motifs and whether there are only two colours in a row or more than two, they may be worked by either the intarsia or the stranding/weaving method. For the patterns shown here, the latter method is generally preferable.

Note, however, that where a colour must be woven across a long distance – as in parts of the Greek key pattern – it is most important to keep the tension very smooth. Also, avoid working the yarn in at the same point on two successive rows, as this will make a visible indentation on the right side.

argyll – 14 rows/16 stitches

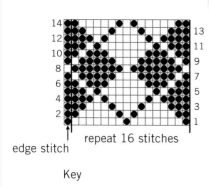

edge stitch   repeat 16 stitches

Key
● A
□ B

dogtooth – 4 rows/4 stitches

repeat
4 stitches

Key
● A
□ B

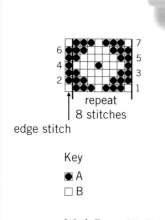

diamond spot – 6 rows/8 stitches

edge stitch

Key
● A
□ B

Work Rows 1 to 7, repeat
Rows 2 to 7.

flower garland – 12 rows/8 stitches

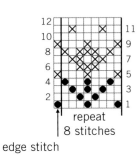

repeat
8 stitches

edge stitch

Key
⊠ A
● B
☐ C

greek key – 20 rows/16 stitches

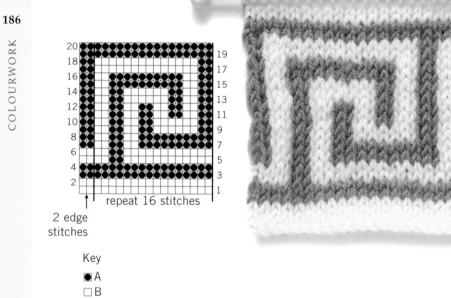

20 19
18 17
16 15
14 13
12 11
10 9
8 7
6 5
4 3
2 1

repeat 16 stitches

2 edge
stitches

Key
⊙ A
☐ B

bird's eye – 8 rows/4 stitches

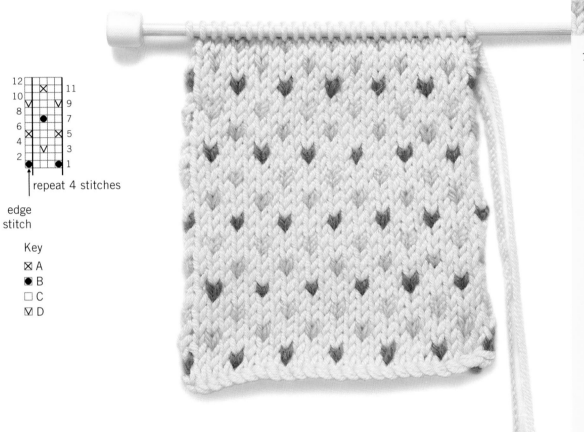

```
12          ×        11
10                    9
 8    ∨       ∨
 6          ●         7
 4    ×       ×        5
 2       ∨            3
      ●       ●       1
```

↑ repeat 4 stitches

edge
stitch

Key
☒ A
◉ B
☐ C
☑ D

colourwork

fair isle patterns

Many beautiful multicoloured patterns have been created on islands off the north coast of Scotland – the Shetlands and the nearby tiny Fair Isle. The motifs are combined and repeated in various ways to make stunning garments.

A sensitive choice of colour is the key to success in working Fair Isle patterns. Ideally, you should use Shetland wool, which is dyed in traditional shades that blend and contrast well. When choosing your yarns, it is a good idea to photocopy the illustration in order to get a black and white representation of the colours. You can then substitute your own colours using a similar balance of lights and darks.

Although the patterns look complex, they actually use only two colours in a row, and are worked using the stranding/weaving technique (see pages 166–169).

cross pattern

repeat
4 stitches

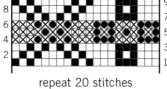

repeat 20 stitches

repeat
4 stitches

Key

□ A
◉ B
■ C
⊠ D

entwined hearts

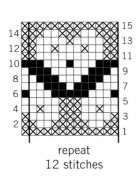

repeat
12 stitches

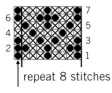

repeat 8 stitches

edge
stitch

Key

⊠ A
◉ B
☐ C
■ D

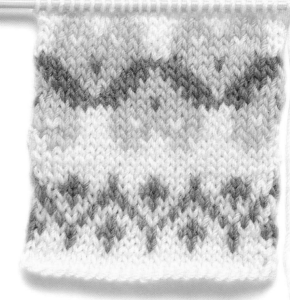

floral band

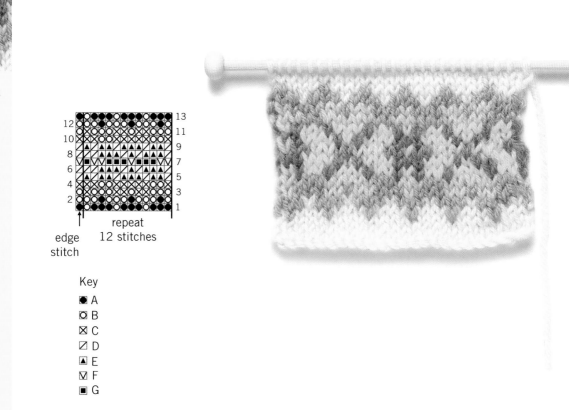

edge
stitch

repeat
12 stitches

Key
- ⬤ A
- ◉ B
- ⊠ C
- ⊿ D
- ▲ E
- ▽ F
- ◼ G

snowflake

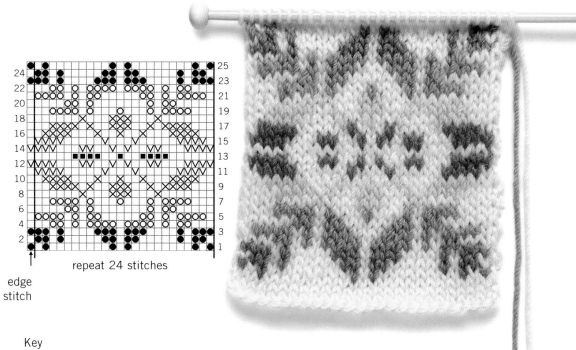

repeat 24 stitches

edge
stitch

Key
- ● A
- ◉ B
- ⊠ C
- ⊽ D
- ▣ E
- ☐ F

heart scroll

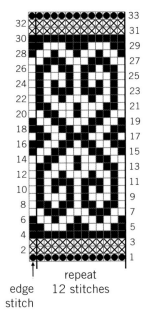

edge
stitch

repeat
12 stitches

Key
- ⬤ A
- ⊠ B
- ⬛ C
- ⬜ D

posy braid

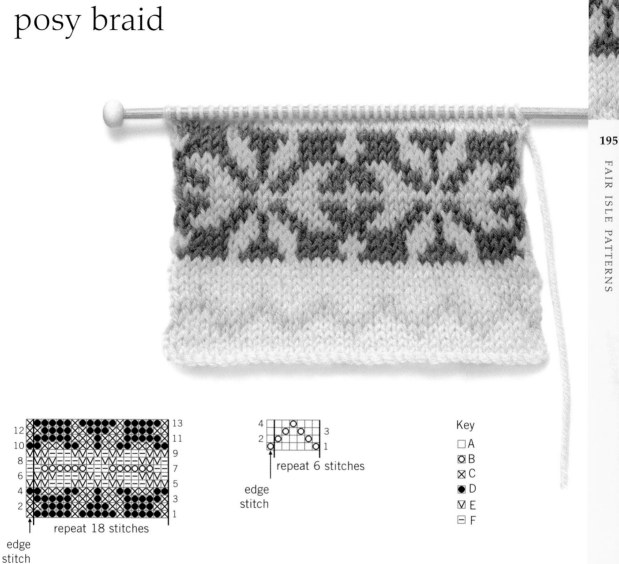

repeat 18 stitches

edge
stitch

13
11
9
7
5
3
1

12
10
8
6
4
2

repeat 6 stitches

edge
stitch

4
2

3
1

Key

☐ A
⊙ B
⊠ C
● D
☑ E
⊟ F

embellishments

Knitting is often embellished in some way. A twisted cord may be required around a waistline or at a neck; a crocheted edging may be used down the front opening of a cardigan; beads, sequins, or embroidery stitches may be worked into the knitting; a deep fringe may be added to a shawl to help it hang gracefully.

Conversely, knitting itself – in the form of a lacy knitted edging – can be used as the embellishment.

In the following few pages you will find instructions for all of these techniques.

decorative cords

Several kinds of decorative cord can be used for drawstrings or decorative ties at a neckline, for example. Experiment with these different kinds of cord, using different types of yarn, to discover their possibilities.

knitted cord

For this cord you will need two double-pointed needles. Only one strand of yarn is used; work with the end of yarn still attached to the ball.

1 Cast on 2 stitches and knit them in the usual way. Without turning the work, move the stitches towards the other end of the needle, bring the yarn firmly from left to right, behind the work, and knit the two stitches.

2 Continue in this way until the cord is the required length. Knit the two stitches together and fasten off. The loose yarn ends can be sewn into the cord, or they can be used to attach a pompom, tassel or bead to each end.

twisted cord

The important thing to remember when making this cord is to twist the strands very tightly indeed, otherwise the finished cord will be flimsy. To estimate how many strands you will need, cut several short strands, twist them together, and then double this twisted length; add or subtract strands as appropriate. Cut the strands for the cord three times the finished length.

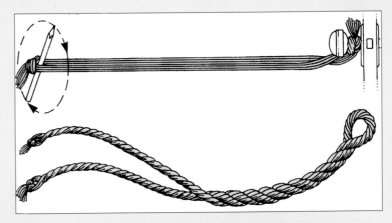

1 Knot the strands together at one end, and anchor this end to a fixed object, such as a doorknob; or ask someone to help you turn from that end.

2 Tie the strands together at the other end, and slip a pencil through the knot.

3 Holding the strands taut, turn the pencil clockwise, continuing to turn until the strands kink up in several places if the tension/gauge is relaxed.

4 Bring the two knotted ends together, and give the cord a firm shake; it will twist around itself. Smooth out the coils, and tie a knot a short distance from the folded end. Also knot the two free ends together. Trim both ends and fluff them out.

plaited cord

Cut the strands slightly longer than the required finished length of the cord, making sure that the number of strands is divisible by 3. Knot the strands together at one end, and pin the knot to a fixed object, such as the upholstered arm of a chair. Plait the strands. Knot the other end and trim the ends if necessary.

trimmings

Many kinds of knitted garment can be decorated with fringes, tassels or pompoms. A simple fringe is the perfect finishing touch for a scarf; a more elaborate knotted one makes an elegant edging on a shawl.

Pompoms make perky trimmings for hats and are favourites on children's garments. A tassel can be sewn to the ends of knitted cords or attached to the four corners of a knitted (or woven fabric) cushion cover.

simple fringe

This fringe is essentially a series of tassels. The strands should be about two and a half times the finished length.

1 Fold the group of strands in half. With the help of a crochet hook, draw the folded end through the edge from front to back.

2 Bring the strands through the loop, and pull downwards gently, bringing the loop up to the edge.

knotted fringe

Elegant lattice-like effects can be created with this technique. The fringe should be at least 12 cm (4½ in) deep; it uses fewer strands than a simple fringe.

1 Knot the strands into the edge of the fabric as for a simple fringe, placing them slightly farther apart.

2 When all the strands have been attached, take half the strands from the first group at one edge and half from the next group, and tie them together as shown. Join the remaining strands from the second group to half the strands from the third group. Continue to the end.

3 On the second row tie the separated strands together. More rows of knotting can be added if desired. An attractive variation is to join some strands with beads.

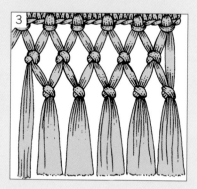

pompoms

To make a pompom, first cut two identical circles from thin cardboard, the diameter of the finished pompom. In the centre of the circles draw another circle, one quarter the diameter of the outer circle. Mark the circle on one piece of cardboard, using any convenient round shape, then mark the smaller circle.

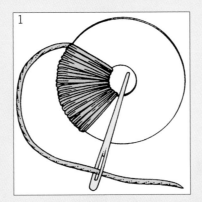

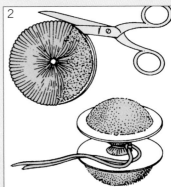

1 Cut a long length of yarn, thread it into a tapestry needle, and wrap the yarn around the two circles. Add more yarn until the hole is tightly filled.

2 With sharp scissors cut around the edge of the circles. Pull the cardboard circles apart slightly and tie a length of yarn firmly around the strands in the middle. Cut away the cardboard circles. Trim any uneven strands.

tassels

From stiff cardboard cut a rectangle the length of the finished tassel.

1 Wind the yarn around the cardboard until the tassel is the desired thickness. Loop a piece of yarn under the strands at one end. Cut through the other end.

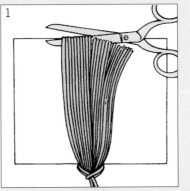

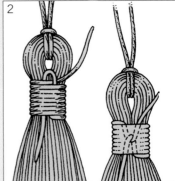

2 Make a loop at one end of a length of yarn; holding the loop alongside the strands, wind the other end around several times.

Slip the free end through the loop. Pull on the two ends to fasten them; trim the ends and push them inside.

beads and sequins

A few beads or sequins can be sewn onto a finished piece of knitting, but if many are required and if they are to be placed evenly over part or all of the garment, they should be knitted in, using one of the methods shown below. When choosing beads or sequins for this purpose, make sure to select ones that have a hole large enough for the yarn to slip through easily, otherwise the yarn is likely to become frayed or even break.

The simpler of the two methods for knitting with beads or sequins is the slipstitch method. The yarn-around-needle method must be used where beads are to be worked into consecutive stitches. Keeping the beads on the right side of the work requires a little more skill than in the slipstitch method. The beads or sequins can be worked into the knit side or purl side of the work. On the wrong side, work fairly tightly to hold the beads in place.

threading beads onto yarn

First thread a sewing needle with a double strand of strong thread as shown. Slip the end of the yarn through the loop of thread, and turn back the end. Thread the beads or sequins onto the yarn, always keeping one bead on the loop to hold it in place.

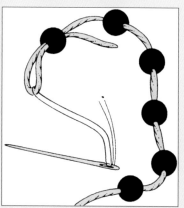

slipstitch method

This method can be used wherever the beads or sequins are separated by at least one stitch. It is normally worked on right-side rows, but can also be worked from the wrong side. At least two rows of knitting should be completed before beads are worked in.

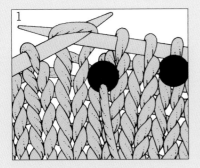 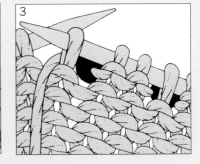

1 Knit up to the position for the bead. Bring the yarn forward and slip the next stitch knitwise.

2 Push the bead up and knit the next stitch. If working a wrong-side row, take the yarn back to the right side of the work, slip the next stitch purlwise.

3 Push the bead up so that it lies close to the right side, and purl the next stitch.

yarn-around-needle method

 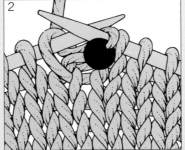 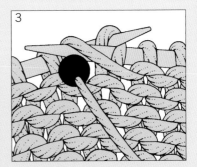

1 On a right-side (knit) row, insert the needle through the back of the next stitch and push a bead up close to the work.

2 Take the yarn around the needle, and push the bead through the stitch to the front. Complete the stitch.

3 On a wrong-side (purl) row, insert the needle purlwise through the back of the loop. Push the bead through the loop.

crochet

A knowledge of elementary crochet techniques is extremely useful for the knitter. Crochet can be used to make simple button loops – often required on baby garments – and to finish edges. It is also sometimes used to join seams.

Crochet is not difficult to learn. Only one implement is required, and mistakes are easily corrected; you simply unravel the work back to the mistake, slip the hook into the loop, and continue.

How to hold the hook and yarn is shown here. The yarn goes around the left little finger, under the second and third finger then over the first finger.

working a chain
The chain (abbreviated ch) is the basic stitch of crochet. A given number of chain stitches are used to begin work and are the equivalent of casting on in knitting.

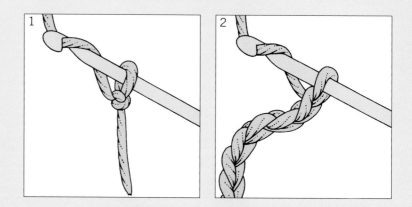

1 Begin with a slip knot. Leave the hook in the loop, and grasp the base of the knot with the left thumb and forefinger. Slide the hook forward under the tensioned yarn and turn it anti/counter clockwise, catching up the yarn as shown.

2 Still keeping the yarn tensioned, pull the hook back through the loop. A new loop has been formed. Repeat steps 1 and 2 to make the required number of chains.

slip stitch

This stitch (abbreviated sl st) is
the shallowest crochet stitch. It
is used to join chain to make a
ring and also to join two pieces
that have already been edged
with double crochet. (Slip stitch
is also sometimes called single
crochet.) Insert the hook into the
top of the stitch (or into a chain
stitch). Draw a loop through the
stitch and through the loop on
the hook in one movement.

double crochet

This stitch (abbreviated dc)
can be worked on a completed
knitted fabric to provide a neat,
firm edge, perhaps in a
contrasting colour.

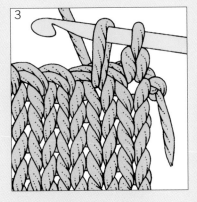

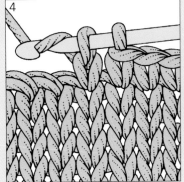

1 Fasten the yarn to the RH
   corner of the work. Insert the
   hook into the first stitch from
   front to back, and draw
   through a loop.

2 Take the yarn around the hook
   and draw this loop through the
   first loop.

3 Insert the hook into the next
   stitch and draw through a
   loop. Two loops are now on
   the hook.

4 Take the yarn around the hook
   and draw it through both
   loops. One double crochet has
   been completed. Repeat steps
   3 and 4 as required. To turn a
   corner, work 3 double crochet
   into the corner stitch.

embroidery on knitting

Embroidery stitches can be used to add motifs to a piece of plain knitting or to enhance or accentuate a stitch pattern.

By far the most commonly used embroidery technique in knitting is Swiss darning. This is worked on a stocking/stockinette stitch fabric and gives the appearance of having been knitted in. Motifs for Swiss darning are normally given in chart form, with one square of the chart representing each stitch. A cross-stitch motif can also be used.

Embroidery on knitting is always worked with a tapestry needle to avoid splitting the yarn. Either a knitting yarn or embroidery thread can be used; the only criterion is that the thread should be appropriate in weight and texture for the background and to the technique used. It is important to stitch with an easy tension to preserve the elasticity of the fabric. Practise first on a spare swatch of the knitting.

swiss darning

Use a single strand of yarn, the same weight and type as that used for the knitting. Begin at the bottom RH corner of the motif, and fasten the yarn with one or two stitches at the back of the area to be covered with the embroidery. Bring the needle up through the base of the first stitch to be embroidered.

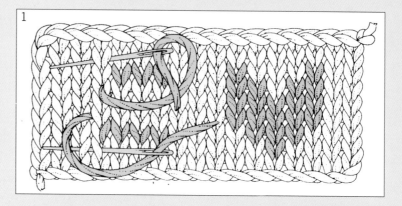

1 Take the needle up to the right, along over the stitch, then under it from right to left, bringing it out as shown in the upper left of the drawing.

2 Take the needle down at the centre of the stitch, where it emerged, and then one stitch to the left as shown in the lower left of the drawing. Repeat steps 1 and 2 to cover this and all subsequent stitches. Take care not to pull the stitches tightly.

cross stitch

This stitch, too, is well suited to a stocking/stockinette stitch fabric. The yarn used should be somewhat thinner than that used for the knitting. Depending on the scale of the work, it is best to work over groups of four stitches. Fasten the yarn on the wrong side.

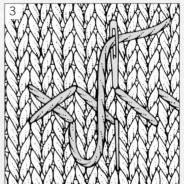

1 Bring the needle up at the lower RH corner of the area to be covered with the stitch, and take it down at the upper LH.

2 Bring it up at the lower LH corner and take it down at the upper RH corner. This completes the stitch.

3 When working cross stitch it is important that all the lower stitches slant in one direction and all the top stitches in another. Therefore, it is better to work in rows, in two stages.

chain stitch

This versatile stitch can be used to work lines in any direction. By varying the thickness of yarn and the spacing of stitches, you can produce quite different effects.

1 Bring the needle up to the right side of the work, form the thread into a small loop, and take the needle back down into the fabric and up inside the loop (top). Pull the thread

gently to tighten the loop. Continue forming loops in this way along the line of stitching. Fasten the last loop by taking the needle down into the fabric just outside the loop (bottom).

2 Individual chain stitches can be worked in a circle to suggest the petals of a flower; in this form the stitch is called 'lazy daisy'. They can also be scattered over the surface.

french knots

It is usually better to choose a yarn at least as thick as that used for the knitting, so that the knots will stand out prominently on the surface.

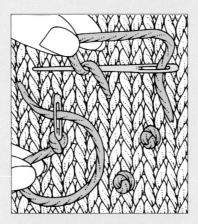

Bring the needle up at the point for the knot. Holding the yarn taut, wrap it once around the needle, close to the place where it emerged, then take the needle to the wrong side, just beside the starting point.

The trick in working a French knot is to take the needle through quickly, so that the thread does not have a chance to unwind. For a larger knot, take the thread twice around the needle.

buttonhole stitch

Also known as blanket stitch, this is a very useful stitch as well as a decorative one. The stitches can be spaced as shown or close together. The vertical legs can be of different lengths, producing an interesting random effect.

1 Work from left to right. Take the needle to the right, to the desired width of the stitch, then insert it above this point at the desired depth (top). Loop the thread around to the right and bring the needle up over it on the lower stitching line. This completes the stitch (bottom). Continue working to the right in this way.

2 Buttonhole stitch can also be worked in circles to produce stylized flower shapes.

couching

This stitch can be used to decorate a knitted fabric with threads that would be difficult or impossible to sew through the fabric. Use a fine sewing thread for the stitching.

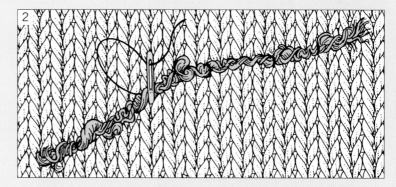

1 Lay the main thread on top of the knitting, leaving a short end free. Bring the stitching thread to the right side, a little beyond the point where the couched thread will be fastened. Take it over the couched thread and back into the fabric.

2 Make another stitch about 1 cm (½ in) farther along the stitching line. Continue in this way. After the last stitch, fasten the working thread on the wrong side.

3 Use a large tapestry needle to take each end of the couched thread to the wrong side. Using fine thread, sew the ends in place.

smocking

As an alternative to knitting in smocking (see page 109), you can embroider the smocking on a knitted fabric. The yarn used for the smocking can be the knitting yarn or an embroidery thread. Work the fabric in a K1, P3 rib.

1 Secure the smocking thread at the lower RH corner, to the left of the second rib.

2 Take it back over the first rib and up again at the starting point, drawing the two ribs together.

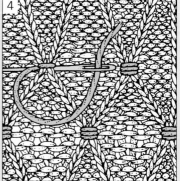

3 Work 2 more backstitches over the ribs, then take the thread under the work and bring it up to the left of the fourth rib.

4 Join the third and fourth ribs in the same way. Work to the end. Work the next row above the first, joining different ribs.

embellishments

edgings

It is important that edgings are the right length for their garments. In the case of an edging worked sideways, the best approach is to work it until it is about 4 cm (1½ in) shorter than the edge to which it will be attached. Without breaking the yarn, slip the stitches onto a safety pin. Sew the edging on as far as possible, then continue knitting until it fits exactly. If the edging is worked from the outer edge inwards, it is necessary to make a sample first; block this, and then calculate the length of the finished edge.

The edging may be sewn on with slipstitch, using sewing thread. One that is worked inwards may be grafted to a knitted edge (see page 226). Knit the last row of the edging, rather than casting/binding off, making sure that the number of stitches matches that on the other edge.

leaf edging

This edging is worked sideways.
Cast on 8 sts.
Row 1 (RS) K5, yf, K1, yf, K2.
Row 2 P6, K into front and back
of next st, K3.
Row 3 K4, P1, K2, yf, K1, yf, K3.
Row 4 P8, K into front and back
of next st, K4.
Row 5 K4, P2, K3, yf, K1, yf, K4.
Row 6 P10, K into front and back
of next st, K5.
Row 7 K4, P3, K4, yf, K1, yf, K5.
Row 8 P12, K into front and back
of next st, K6.
Row 9 K4, P4, sl 1, K1, psso, K7,
K2 tog, K1.
Row 10 P10, K into front and back
of next st, K7.
Row 11 K4, P5, sl 1, K1, psso, K5,
K2 tog, K1.
Row 12 P8, K into front and back
of next st, K2, P1, K5.
Row 13 K4, P1, K1, P4, sl 1, K1,
psso, K3, K2 tog, K1.
Row 14 P6, K into front and back
of next st, K3, P1, K5.
Row 15 K4, P1, K1, P5, sl 1, K1,
psso, K1, K2 tog, K1.
Row 16 P4, K into front and back
of next st, K4, P1, K5.
Row 17 K4, P1, K1, P6, sl 1, K2 tog,
psso, K1.

Row 18 P2 tog, cast/bind off
5 sts kw using P2 tog to cast/bind
off first st, P3, K4.
8 sts remain.

faggot and scallop edging

This edging is worked sideways.
Cast on 13 sts.
Row 1 K7, yf, sl 1, K1, psso, yf, K4.
Row 2 K2, P10, K2.
Row 3 K6, (yf, sl 1, K1, psso)
twice, yf, K4.
Row 4 K2, P11, K2.
Row 5 K5, (yf, sl 1, K1, psso)
3 times, yf, K4.
Row 6 K2, P12, K2.
Row 7 K4, (yf, sl 1, K1, psso)
4 times, yf, K4.
Row 8 K2, P13, K2.
Row 9 K3, (yf, sl 1, K1, psso)
5 times, yf, K4.
Row 10 K2, P14, K2.
Row 11 K4, (yf, sl 1, K1, psso)
5 times, K2 tog, K2.
Row 12 K2, P13, K2.
Row 13 K5, (yf, sl 1, K1, psso)
4 times, K2 tog, K2.
Row 14 K2, P12, K2.
Row 15 K6, (yf, sl 1, K1, psso)
3 times, K2 tog, K2.
Row 16 K2, P11, K2
Row 17 K7, (yf, sl 1, K1, psso)
twice, K2 tog, K2.
Row 18 K2, P10, K2.
Row 19 K8, yf, sl 1, K1, psso,
K2 tog, K2.
Row 20 K2, P9, K2.

godmother's edging

This edging is worked sideways.

Cast on 20 sts.

Row 1 (WS) K.

Row 2 Sl 1, K3, (yf, K2 tog) 7 times, yf, K2.

Rows 3, 5, 7, and 9 K.

Row 4 Sl 1, K6, (yf, K2 tog) 6 times, yf, K2.

Row 6 Sl 1, K9, (yf, K2 tog) 5 times, yf, K2.

Row 8 Sl 1, K12, (yf, K2 tog) 4 times, yf, K2.

Row 10 Sl 1, K23.

Row 11 Cast (bind) off 4 sts, K19.

20 sts remain.

Rep rows 2–11.

seashore edging

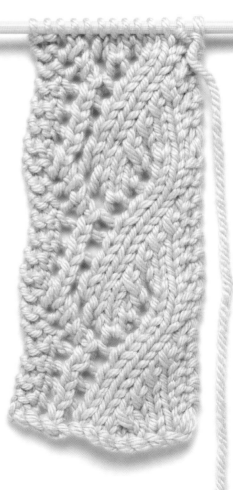

This edging is worked sideways.
Cast on 13 sts.
Row 1 (RS) Sl 1, K3, yf, K5, yf,
K2 tog, yf, K2.
Row 2 K2, P11, K2.
Row 3 Sl 1, K4, sl 1, K2 tog, psso,
K2, (yf, K2 tog) twice, K1.
Row 4 K2, P9, K2.
Row 5 Sl 1, K3, sl 1, K1, psso, K2,
(yf, K2 tog) twice, K1.
Row 6 K2, P8, K2.
Row 7 Sl 1, K2, sl 1, K1, psso, K2,
(yf, K2 tog) twice, K1.
Row 8 K2, P7, K2.
Row 9 Sl 1, K1, sl 1, K1, psso, K2,
(yf, K2 tog) twice, K1.
Row 10 K2, P6, K2.
Row 11 Sl 1, sl 1, K1, psso, K2, yf,
K1, yf, K2 tog, yf, K2.
Row 12 K2, P7, K2.
Row 13 Sl 1, (K3, yf) twice,
K2 tog, yf, K2.
Row 14 K2, P9, K2.

special techniques

The skills covered here include some that you may need only occasionally, such as inserting a zip fastener/zipper or working a knitted-in hem, as well as skills that will give your knitting a professional touch; these include such refinements as a bias cast/bind-off for slanting shoulder seams, an invisible cast-on edge, how to join knitted edges by grafting, rather than sewing them together, and several different kinds of hems and pockets.

As you gain experience and confidence as a knitter, you will often find that you can improve on the techniques specified in a commercial pattern. For example, you might wish to knit a patch pocket on picked-up stitches, rather than sewing it on. Practise these special techniques and keep the samples for reference later.

advanced casting on

The two methods of casting on shown here are well worth learning. They are often called 'invisible' casting-on methods because they employ a separate length of yarn which is later removed.

Method 1 is used on a single rib fabric; when the foundation yarn is removed, the edge that remains appears to consist only of ribbing, although the first four rows are actually produced by a slipstitch technique. The smooth edge is flexible and attractive, and worth the small amount of extra work involved.

In Method 2 the edge that remains consists of loose stitches which can either be picked up and knitted (for a lacy edging perhaps) or grafted to another edge for an invisible join.

The edge produced by the invisible cast-on (Method 1) is flexible, attractive and hard-wearing.

invisible cast-on – method 1

This method is used for a single ribbing, worked over an odd number of stitches. A contrasting yarn (later removed) is used for the initial cast-on.

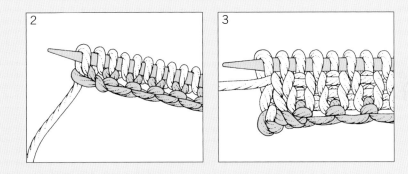

1 Using the thumb or double cast-on method (easier to remove than the cable method), cast onto the needle half the number of stitches that will be required, rounding the result up to the next number. Thus, if 53 stitches will be needed, you should cast on 27 (rounded up from 26½).

2 Join on the main yarn and cut off the contrasting yarn. Work the first 5 rows as follows:
Row 1 (inc row) K1, *yf, K1, rep from * to end. The correct number of sts should now be on the needle.

3 **Row 2** Wyf sl 1 pw, *K1, wyf sl 1 pw, rep from * to end.
Row 3 K1, *wyf sl 1 purlwise, K1, rep from * to end.
Row 4 as row 2.
Row 5 as row 3.

4 Now work in K1, P1 rib for the required depth. Unpick the contrasting yarn.

invisible cast-on – method 2

A contrasting yarn, of any colour, is used in this method; it is removed later.

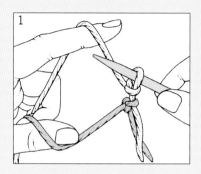

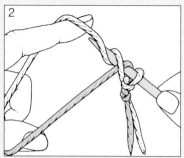

1 Make a slip knot in the main yarn (called A) and place it on the needle. Tie the contrasting yarn (called B) to the main yarn, and hold the two yarns in the left hand as shown. Take yarn A over the needle from front to back.

2 Take yarn B over the needle from back to front. The yarns are now crossed on top of the needle.

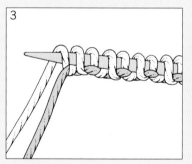

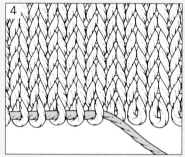

3 Take yarn A over the needle again from front to back, and pull both yarns around the far side of the needle, so bringing them below it. Recite to yourself, 'front to back, back to front, front to back and down'. The contrasting yarn should lie in a straight line along the lower edge of the cast-on stitches.

4 When the required number of stitches have been cast on, tie the contrasting yarn to the main yarn at the end, and cut it off. Leave this yarn in place until the knitting is completed, then remove it and pick up the stitches as instructed by the pattern for further knitting or grafting.

multiple increase

Some patterns will require you to cast on a number of stitches at a side edge in order to work some shaping – for example to add a sleeve on a T-shaped garment. Any convenient cast-on method can be used for this; however, if you are using a two-strand method, such as the double cast-on, you will need to tie an extra strand onto the work.

If the increase is to be made at the left-hand edge of the garment (that is, the left edge with the work facing you), the extra stitches are cast on immediately after completing a right-side row, so that the first row worked on them will be a wrong-side row. If the increase is to come at the right-hand edge, the stitches are cast on after completing a wrong-side row.

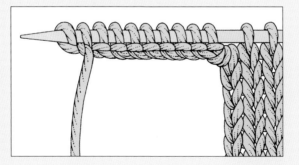

advanced casting/binding off

Here are four different ways of casting/binding off to add to your repertoire of knitting techniques.

The suspended cast/bind-off is a very useful method, as it is more flexible than the basic method (see page 28). It can be used on ribbing (although the edge is somewhat more conspicuous than a rib cast/bind-off or wherever elasticity is important.

The bias cast/bind-off is not a true cast/bind-off method, but a special way of shaping an edge that would otherwise be cast/bound off on alternate rows, in stages, producing a stepped effect.

The double cast/bind-off bind-off can be used to join a shoulder seam or any other straight edges having the same number of stitches. It makes the perfect finishing touch to a bias cast/bind-off.

The invisible cast/bind-off is the trickiest method; however, it is ideal on a piece of single ribbing – where an inconspicuous finish is desired.

suspended cast/bind-off

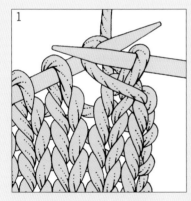  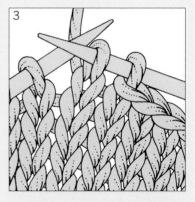

1 Work the first 2 stitches. * Lift the first stitch over the second, as usual, but leave the lifted stitch on the LH needle.

2 Still leaving the first 2 stitches in place, work the third stitch.

3 Drop the second and third stitches off the LH needle. Two loops are now on the RH needle. Repeat from * until 2 stitches remain; knit these together.

bias cast/bind-off

A pattern will normally instruct you to cast/bind off in stages and will give the exact number of stitches to be cast/bound off on each shaping row. The process will typically take 5 rows. You can easily convert the instructions to make a bias cast/bind-off, as described below. The illustrations here show a cast/bind-off on the LH edge.

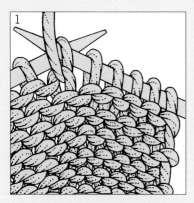

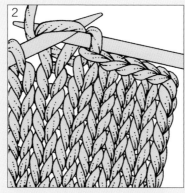

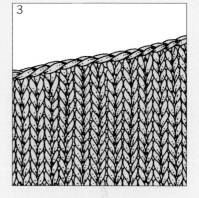

1 Work up to the last row before the shoulder shaping, ending at the neck edge with a wrong-side row. Work across the stitches up to those to be cast/bound off. Turn, leaving these stitches unworked. Slip the first stitch purlwise.

2 Work across to the end (neck edge). Turn and work across the stitches up to the next group to be cast/bound off. Turn, leaving these stitches unworked. Slip the first stitch purlwise. Work across to the end. Continue in this way until only the last group of stitches remains to be worked. With the right side facing, cast/bind-off all the stitches.

3 The cast/bind-off edge slopes smoothly. To cast/bind off a RH edge, work as above, reversing the terms 'right side' and 'wrong side'.

double cast/bind-off

This is a combined cast/bind-off and seam. The edges to be joined must have exactly the same number of stitches.

Work the two pieces of knitting up to the last row before casting/binding off; leave the stitches on a spare needle. Before working the cast/bind-off, arrange the two pieces on the needles so that when they are placed together with right sides facing the needles will point towards the right.

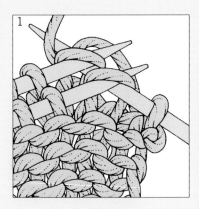

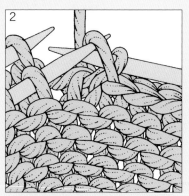

1 Holding the two pieces together, with right sides facing, insert a third needle knitwise through the first stitch on both pieces, and knit the two together. Work the next 2 stitches together in the same way.

2 Using one of the two needles in the left hand (either will do), lift the first stitch over the second, as for the basic cast/bind-off. Repeat steps both steps until all the stitches have been cast/bound off.

The invisible cast/bind-off produces an edge that is ideal for a polo neck – or wherever smooth, flexible, ribbing is especially important.

invisible cast/bind-off

This ingenius method of casting/binding off a single rib fabric may seem dauntingly complex at first; but if you persevere you will be delighted with the results. It makes highly professional finish on a ribbed collar or neckband. To practise cast/bind on an odd number of stitches – at least 25

– and work in K1, P1 rib for about 4 cm (1½ in), ending with a wrong-side row. Cut off the thread, allowing 3 times the width of the knitting, and thread the end into a tapestry needle. In the illustrations this is shown in a contrasting colour for clarity. The knit stitches have been given odd numbers, the purl stitches even ones.

Each stitch is worked into twice; the first time in a direction contrary to its construction, the second time in the same direction. Only then is the stitch slipped off the needle.

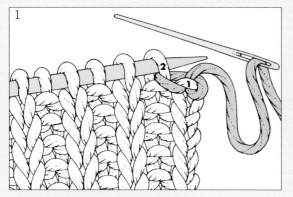

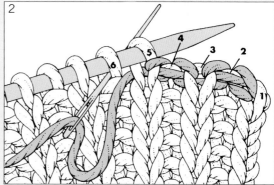

1 To begin, insert the tapestry needle purlwise into stitch 1, then knitwise into stitch 2. Leave these stitches on the needle. Work knitwise into stitch 1 and slip it off the needle.

2 Work purlwise into stitch 3. Work purlwise into stitch 2 and slip it off the needle. Take the tapestry needle behind stitch 3 and to the front between stitches 3 and 4. Work knitwise into stitch 4. Repeat steps 2–5, working into stitches 3, 5, 4 and 6 . Continue in this way to the end of the row.

grafting

Grafting is a method of sewing two knitted edges together stitch by stitch, so that the join is invisible. The sewing stitches duplicate the structure of the knitting. This technique is often used to join a front and back section at the shoulder. The edges need not be straight, as shown; they could be shaped, as shown on page 223.

To work the grafting, you can either place the pieces on a flat surface, as shown in these illustrations, or hold them together with wrong sides facing and the needles close together in your hand. Grafting can also be used to join an edge that has been cast on using the invisible Method 2 (see page 220).

grafting garter stitch

Although most often used on stocking/stockinette stitch, grafting can be used on other patterns, such as garter stitch.

End one piece on a right-side row, the other on a wrong-side row, so that the lower piece will have a ridge close to the needle and the other piece will have the ridge one row away.

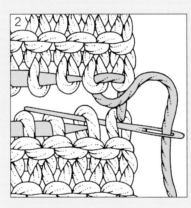
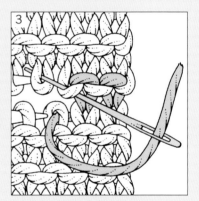

1 Take the needle purlwise through the first stitch on the lower edge, purlwise through the first upper stitch and knitwise through the next upper stitch.

2 * Insert the needle knitwise again through the first lower stitch, then purlwise through the second lower stitch.

3 Insert the needle purlwise through the upper stitch, then knitwise through the next upper stitch. Repeat from * to end.

grafting stocking/stockinette stitch

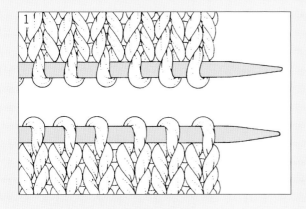

1 End one piece of knitting with a knit row and the other with a purl row, so that when the work is positioned as shown the needles will both point to the right.

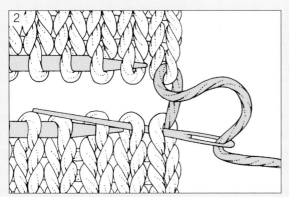

2 Thread a tapestry needle with matching yarn, 3 times the width of the knitted edge. Insert the needle purlwise through the first stitch on the lower edge, then purlwise through the opposite stitch on the upper edge. Take it knitwise through the first stitch again, then purlwise through the second stitch on the same edge.

3 * Insert the needle knitwise into the stitch on the upper edge where the yarn emerges, then purlwise into the next stitch to the left. Insert it knitwise into the stitch just below, then purlwise into the next stitch to the left. Repeat from * to end.

hems, facings and waistbands

Hems are needed wherever a reasonably firm edge that lies flat is required: on the lower and front opening edges of a tailored jacket, for example. A vertical hem is normally called a facing.

It is sometimes possible – when working a skirt, for example – to work from the top downwards, ending with the hem. The hem edge stitches can be cast/bound off, or left on the needle and sewn to the main fabric using the stitch-by-stitch method (see page 230).

Similar to a hem is a knitted waistband. This is often worked in single ribbing and used on garments for babies or toddlers, as the extra-snug fit compensates for the lack of a natural waistline. A less bulky alternative to a knitted waistband is one worked in herringbone stitch.

sewn-in hem with ridge foldline

This hem is best suited to a garment worked in stocking/stockinette stitch. Use a cast-on method with a fairly flat edge. If you plan to use the stitch-by-stitch sewing method (see page 230) for attaching the hem, use the invisible cast-on Method 2 (see page 220). For the hem itself, use needles one or two sizes smaller than those specified for the main fabric. This helps it to lie smoothly when turned up.

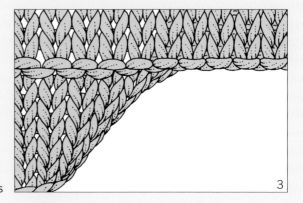

1 Work in stocking/stockinette stitch for the required depth of the hem, ending with a wrong-side row.

2 On the next (right-side) row, purl, rather than knit, to produce a ridge on the fabric. This will serve as the foldline.

3 Change to the larger needles and continue in stocking/stockinette stitch for the main part of the garment.

sewn-in hem with slipstitch foldline

This hem is preferred for garments worked in textured stitch patterns or heavyweight yarn.

1 Work the depth of the hem in stocking/stockinette stitch, using smaller needles, as for the ridge foldline hem, ending with a wrong-side row.

2 On the next (right-side) row, work as follows: *K1, wyf sl 1, rep from * to last st, K1.

3 Change to larger needles and work the main part of the garment in pattern.

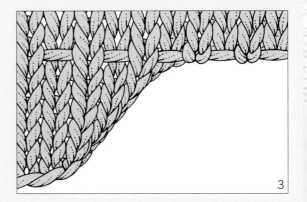

sewn in hem with picot foldline

This hem is best worked in a fine yarn.

1 Cast on an odd number of stitches, and work in stocking/stockinette stitch, using smaller needles, to the desired depth, ending with a wrong-side row.

2 On the next (right-side) row, work as follows: *K2 tog, yf, rep from * to last st, K1.

3 Change to larger needles, and continue in pattern. When completed, turn up the hem along the line of eyelets to produce the picot effect.

whipstitch

This stitch is suitable for sewing up the hem on a garment worked in a light- or medium-weight yarn. Work through a single purled loop of the main fabric, then through a loop on the hem edge as shown.

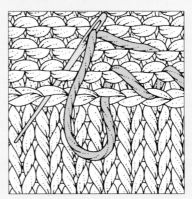

blind hemming stitch

This method is suitable for a heavyweight fabric. You may need to separate the yarn and use one or two plies to reduce bulk. First tack the hem in place, about 1 cm (⅜ in) below the edge. Turn the garment as shown, with the hem fold away from you. Work the stitches between the hem edge and the main fabric so that the hem edge is free.

stitch-by-stitch method

This method can be used on an edge that has been cast on using the invisible Method 2 or on the edge of a section that has been worked from the top down. In the first case, remove the foundation yarn gradually as you work the hem; in the second, leave the needle in the work, removing it as you stitch.

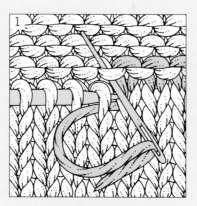

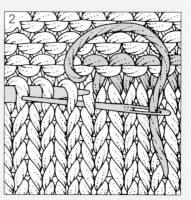

1 Fasten the sewing yarn at the RH edge, and insert the needle purlwise through the first stitch on the lower edge. Take it through the corresponding stitch in the main fabric, then knitwise through the first lower stitch. Insert the needle knitwise through the next stitch on the lower edge, then purlwise into the next stitch above.

2 Continue working in this way to the end.

knitted-in hem

This is an ingenious way of turning up a hem, but it must be worked carefully if it is not to look bulky. Before knitting the garment itself, work a small sample and adjust the hem needle size and the number of rows if necessary. The needles used for the hem should be two or three sizes smaller than those used for the main fabric.

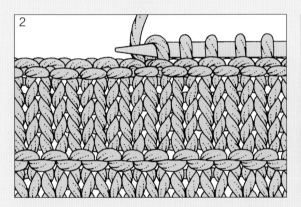

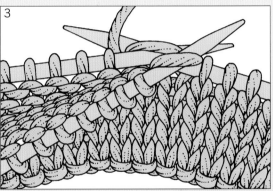

1 Cast on the required number of stitches and work the hem allowance as for a sewn-in hem. Work a ridge or slipstitch foldline, and continue with the larger needles until the main part of the garment is the same depth as the hem allowance, ending with a wrong-side row. Leave the stitches on the needle.

2 Using a spare needle and working on the right side, pick up and knit stitches along the cast-on edge. Work into the farther loop of each stitch – the one that will be closer to the garment. Fasten off the extra yarn.

3 Turn up the hem along the ridge. Using the main yarn and working on the right side of the garment, knit one stitch from the garment together with one stitch from the hem all along the row. The picked-up stitches from the hem are now securely knitted into the main fabric.

vertical facing

A vertical facing may be required on the front edge of a jacket, for example. The facing itself should be worked in stocking/stockinette stitch, whatever the main fabric is worked in. The illustration shows a left front edge; for a right front edge the process is reversed.

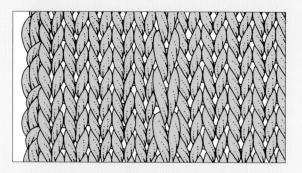

On a right-side row, work in pattern to the foldline; slip the next stitch purlwise; continue in stocking stitch to the end of the row. On a wrong-side row, work in stocking stitch up to and including the slipped stitch; continue in pattern to the end. When the section is complete, turn the facing to the wrong side along the foldline and stitch it in place.

mitred hem and facing

For a neat finish on the lower edges of a jacket, work a hem and facing with a mitred corner. First calculate, from the garment tension/gauge, the number of stitches to cast on for the hem. Find the number of stitches in 2.5 cm (1 in), and subtract this from the number required for the full width of the section.

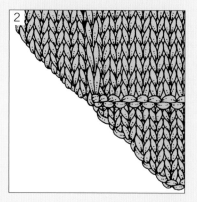

1 Cast on the reduced number of stitches and work in stocking/stockinette stitch, increasing 1 stitch at the front edge on every alternate row until the total number are on the needle.

2 Work the turning ridge, then continue increasing, working a slipstitch foldline (above). When the facing is the same depth as the hem, work straight.

3 When the knitting is complete, oversew the diagonal edges neatly together.

herringbone casing

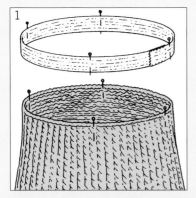

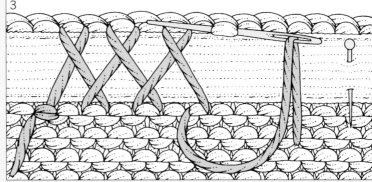

1 Join the elastic to form a ring, first making sure that it fits the waist smoothly without stretching. Divide the elastic into 4 equal sections and mark them with pins. Similarly mark the 4 quarters of the skirt edge.

2 Pin the elastic to the wrong side of the waist edge, matching the points.

3 Fasten the knitting yarn to the fabric with two backstitches, just below the elastic. Take it up over the elastic and to the right, and insert the needle through the edge of the knitting from right to left. Take it down to the right and insert it again from the left. Continue around the waistband; fasten off securely.

knitted waistband

1 Work a ridge foldline as shown on page 228, then knit the waistband in K1, P1 rib until it is the required depth.

2 Sew the waistband in place, leaving about 5 cm (2 in) unstitched.

3 Thread elastic through the casing, and pin the ends together with a safety pin. Check the fit. Sew the ends together firmly, then complete the stitching on the casing edge.

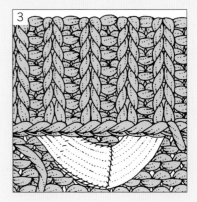

pockets

The three most popular styles of pocket are the patch pocket, the horizontal inside pocket and the vertical inside pocket. There are various methods of working these different types; you can often substitute a method you prefer for the one in a pattern.

Patch pockets are usually most successful in a textured stitch pattern, which provides contrast. A stocking/stockinette stitch patch pocket can have a homemade look if it is not sewn on very carefully. If a stocking/stockinette stitch pocket is required, a neat way of attaching it is with Swiss darning. Another option is to work a modified patch pocket on stitches picked up from the main fabric. Working a garter stitch selvedge along the two sides will provide a neat finish.

A patch pocket can be attached with one of the side edges left unstitched, instead of the top edge, to make a vertical patch pocket.

swiss-darned patch pocket

1 Work the patch to the desired size and cast/bind off. Block or press it as appropriate, and darn in the ends. Pin the pocket to the garment. Fasten the yarn (shown here in a contrasting colour for clarity) at the lower RH corner on the wrong side of the main fabric, and bring it up in the centre of the first stitch in from the edge as shown.

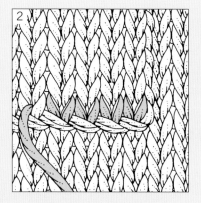

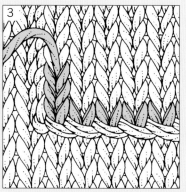

2 Work Swiss darning (see page 206) over all the stitches across the lower edge of the pocket.

3 Continue up the LH side of the pocket as shown. Fasten off. Swiss-darn the RH edge of the pocket in the same way.

patch pocket on picked-up stitches

This style of pocket, too, is worked after the main section has been completed.

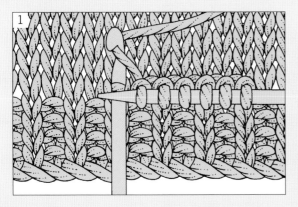

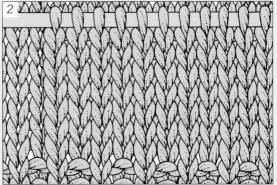

1 Fasten the yarn on the wrong side of the work at the position of the lower RH corner of the pocket. Using a crochet hook, pick up the required number of stitches for the pocket and place them on the needle.

2 Beginning with a purl row, work in stocking/ stockinette stitch to the required depth for the pocket. Cast/bind off evenly.

3 Sew the side edges of the pocket in place, either with Swiss darning or with oversewing.

oversewing a patch pocket

1 Lay the pocket on the main section, and insert a pin diagonally at each corner, through the background fabric only. Remove the pocket, and check that the pins are aligned on the same vertical and horizontal rows.

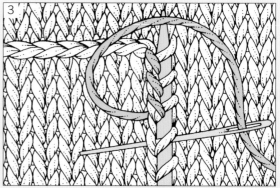

2 Take two fine double-pointed needles and insert them in the fabric between the pins, picking up alternate stitches.

3 Place the pocket between the needles, and oversew it to the picked-up stitches, working into the alternating stitches along the pocket edge. When both sides have been sewn, oversew the lower edge in place, again working through alternate stitches.

horizontal inside pocket

A pattern will often instruct you to place a horizontal pocket by leaving the stitches for the border on a spare needle, joining in the pocket lining and then picking up the opening stitches and working the border. The following method incorporates the border stitches in the fabric, producing a slightly neater finish.

1 First work the pocket lining, casting on 2 more stitches than are allowed for the opening. Work the lining to the required depth, ending with a knit row and decreasing 1 stitch at each end of the previous purl row. Leave the stitches on a spare needle.

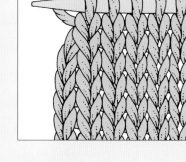

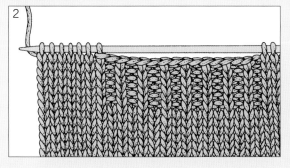

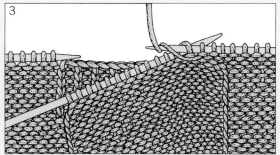

2 Work the main fabric up to the position for the pocket border. Continue knitting, working the border in the chosen pattern. When the border is the required depth, cast/bind off these stitches on a right-side row; work to the end.

3 On the next row, purl across to the beginning of the pocket opening, then purl across the stitches of the pocket lining and continue to the end of the row.

4 When the section is complete, oversew the pocket lining edges in place on the wrong side.

vertical pocket with borders included

The opening for a vertical pocket is worked in two stages, first one side and then the other. When the second side is as deep as the first, the two sides are rejoined. A pocket lining is incorporated in the outer side section of the fabric.

The border of a vertical pocket can either be knitted along with the top part of the pocket or worked later on picked-up stitches as shown below. The illustrations show a pocket in the right side of a garment. For the left side, reverse the instructions.

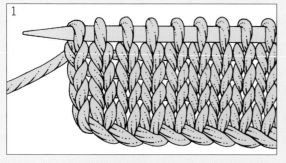

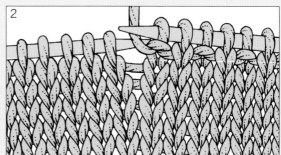

1 Work a few rows of stocking/stockinette stitch for the lower part of the pocket lining. End with a right-side row, and place the stitches on a spare needle.

2 Work the main section up to the level for the pocket opening, ending with a wrong-side row. On the next row, work across to the inner edge of the border, then work in the border pattern across the specified number of stitches. Slip the remaining stitches for the outer side section onto a spare needle.

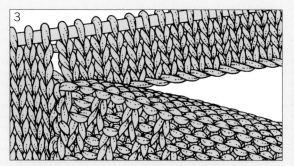

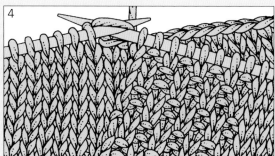

3 Continue working on the top section of the pocket until it is the required depth, ending with a right-side row. Slip these stitches onto a spare needle; do not break off the yarn. Now pick up the pocket lining; place it alongside the outer side section, join on new yarn if necessary, and knit to the end of the row.

4 Continue working across the outer side section and pocket lining until this piece is one row shorter than the top section, ending with a wrong-side row. On the next row, cast/bind off the pocket lining stitches. Rejoin the two sections of the main fabric; and knit to the end of the row.

5 When the section is complete, sew the pocket lining to the main fabric with whipstitch.

vertical pocket with border added

Work this pocket as for the one with a knitted border, but do not work the border stitches. (The division should be placed slightly closer to the centre front.) When the section is completed, pick up stitches along the edge of the top section of the pocket and work in the chosen pattern. Sew the edges to the main fabric.

fastenings

Fastenings can be problematical in a knitted garment because the fabric is soft and stretchy and is inclined to pull away from a zip/zipper or buttons.

    When inserting a zip/zipper, it is important to provide a firm edge for the zip/zipper opening. If the knitting is in a heavyweight yarn, this is best done by working a selvedge; on lightweight knitting, use crochet.

inserting a zip/zipper – selvedge opening

When working the garment, add 2 stitches to the opening edges, and work a double garter stitch selvedge (see page 55). Block or press the completed sections.

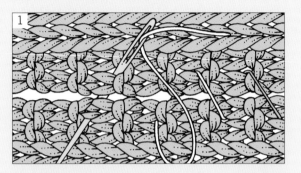

1 Place the adjacent sections right side up, and tack them together using an oversewing stitch and a tapestry needle.

2 Turn the work wrong side upwards. Open the zip/zipper and place it over the opening with the teeth exactly centred. Using an ordinary sewing needle, tack the zip/zipper tape to the knitting down one side. Close the zip/zipper; continue tacking up the other side.

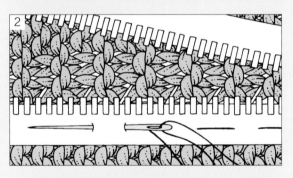

3 Working from the right side and using strong sewing thread such as buttonhole twist, sew the zip/zipper in place with backstitch. Start at the top and work down side and up the other.

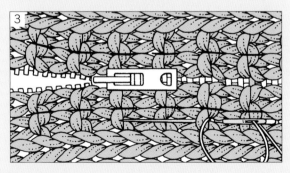

crocheted zip/zipper opening

1 Before sewing in the zip/zipper, work a row of double crochet (see page 205) along the opening edges.

2 Tack and stitch the zip/zipper in place as described for a selvedge opening, working the backstitch along the outer edge of the crochet.

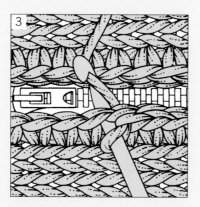

3 Open the zip/zipper and work slip stitches (see page 205) into the double crochet.

ribbon-faced buttonhole band

To prevent the button and buttonhole bands of a cardigan from sagging, sew a length of ribbon (grosgrain is the usual choice, but any firm ribbon will do) to the underside of the bands.

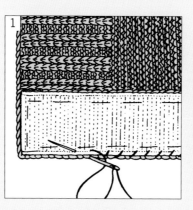

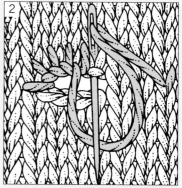

1 Cut the ribbon about 3 cm (1¼ in) longer than the band. Turn under one end and tack it to the knitting; trim the other end if necessary, and turn it under. Slipstitch the ribbon in place as shown.

2 To finish, turn the buttonhole band right side and cut a slit in the ribbon under each buttonhole, taking care not to cut into the knitting. Using yarn or matching perlé cotton and a chenille needle (a large-eyed sharp-pointed embroidery needle), work buttonhole stitch around the buttonholes.

special techniques
ribbon patterns

Among the most intriguing of knitting stitch patterns are those
in which smooth, ribbon-like bands of stocking/stockinette stitch
form zigzag, plaited or woven effects. A simple basketweave
pattern is shown on page 38. Here are some patterns offering
more of a challenge and a more dramatic effect.

    The zigzag ribbon pattern is relatively simple, but creates
a wonderful *trompe l'oeil* texture. Double wing openwork
combines the ribbon-like motif with the delicacy of lace.
Ribbon lattice is a striking pattern which has considerable
impact when worked in a large piece. But the 'star turn' for any
knitter is surely the *entrelacs* pattern (a French word meaning
'interlaced'). It is certainly complex – but worth the effort!

zigzag ribbon pattern

multiple of 11 plus 2

Row 1 (RS) K1, *P1, K10, rep from * to last st, K1.

Row 2 K1, *P9, K2, rep from * to last st, K1.

Row 3 K1, *P3, K8, rep from * to last st, K1.

Row 4 K1, *P7, K4, rep from * to last st, K1.

Row 5 K1, *P5, K6, rep from * to last st, K1.

Rows 6 and 7 As Row 5.

Row 8 as Row 4.

Row 9 as Row 3.

Row 10 as Row 2.

Row 11 as Row 1.

Row 12 K1, *K1, P10, rep from * to last st, K1.

Row 13 K1, *K9, P2, rep from * to last st, K1.

Row 14 K1, *K3, P8, rep from * to last st, K1.

Row 15 K1, *K7, P4, rep from * to last st, K1.

Row 16 K1, *K5, P6, rep from * to last st, K1.

Rows 17 and 18 As Row 16.

Row 19 as Row 15.

Row 20 as Row 14.

Row 21 as Row 13.

Row 22 as Row 12.

double wing openwork

multiple of 16
Row 1 (RS) K.
Row 2 *K4, P8, K4, rep from *.
Row 3 *P3, K2 tog, K3, yf and around needle twice, K3, sl 1, K1, psso, P3, rep from *.
Row 4 *K3, P4, purl into front and back of extra loop, P4, K3, rep from *.

Row 5 *P2, K2 tog, K3, yf, K2, yf, K3, sl 1, K1, psso, P2, rep from *.
Row 6 *K2, P12, K2, rep from *.
Row 7 *P1, K2 tog, K3, yf, K4, yf, K3, sl 1, K1, psso, P1, rep from *.
Row 8 *K1, P14, K1, rep from *.
Row 9 *K2 tog, K3, yf, K6, yf, K3, sl 1, K1, psso, rep from *.
Row 10 P.

entrelacs pattern

multiple of 6

Note Colour A = fawn, Colour B = brown, Colour C = beige. Join in and break off yarns where necessary.

Foundation Row (base triangles) With A, *P2, turn and K2, turn and P3, turn and K3, turn and P4, turn and K4, turn and P5, turn and K5, turn and P6, rep from *. Cont in stripe sequence of 1 row in B, 1 row in C, and 1 row in A, as follows:

Row 1 (RS) K2, turn and P2, turn and inc in first st, sl 1, K1, psso, turn and P3, turn and inc in first st, K1, sl 1, K1, psso, turn and P4, turn and inc in first st, K2, sl 1, K1, psso, turn and P5, turn and inc in first st, K3, sl 1, K1, psso (edge triangle complete), then cont as follows: *K up 6 sts down side edge of same section of previous row; working across these sts and next 6 sts on LH needle, cont as follows: (turn and P6, turn and K5, sl 1, K1, psso) 6 times, rep from * to last section, K up 6 sts down side edge of last section, turn and P2 tog, P4, turn and K5, turn and P2 tog, P3, turn and K4, turn and P2 tog, P2, turn and K3, turn and P2 tog, P1, turn and K2, turn and P2 tog, Fasten off.

Row 2 *With WS facing, pick up and P 6 sts down side edge of first section of previous row and working across these sts, and next 6 sts on LH needle, cont as follows: (turn and K6, turn and P5, P2 tog) 6 times, rep from *.

Keeping stripe sequence correct, rep Rows 1 and 2 for the required depth, ending with Row 1.

Next row (finishing row) *With WS facing, pick up and P6 sts down side edge of first section of previous row. Working across these sts and next 6 sts on LH needle, cont as follows: turn and K6, turn and P2 tog, P3, P2 tog, turn and K5, turn and P2 tog, P2, P2 tog, turn and K4, turn and P2 tog, P1, P3 tog, turn and K3, turn and P2 tog, P3 tog turn and K2, turn and P2 tog. Fasten off. Rep from *.

ribbon lattice pattern

multiple of 18 plus 1 extra
Note 'Kfb': K into front and back of st.
In this pattern the number of sts varies from row to row. Accurate count of sts may be made on any row, apart from Rows 9–12 and 25–28.
Row 1 (RS) *K3, K2 tog, K4, (K1, yf, K1) into next st, K4, sl 1,K1, psso, K2, rep from * to last st, K1.
Row 2 K1, *K2, P6, K1, P6, K3, rep from *.
Row 3 *K2, K2 tog, K5, yf, K1, yf, K5, sl 1, K1, psso, K1, rep from * to last st, K1.
Row 4 K1, *K1, P6, K3, P6, K2, rep from *.
Row 5 *K1, K2 tog, K5, yf, K3, yf, K5, sl 1,K1, psso, rep from * to last st, K1.
Row 6 K1, *P6, K5, P6, K1, rep from *.
Row 7 K2 tog, *K5, (yf, K5) twice, sl 1, K2 tog, psso, rep from * ending last rep sl 1, K1, psso instead of sl 1, K2 tog, psso.
Row 8 P1, *P5, K7, P6, rep from *.
Row 9 Kfb, *sl 1, K1, psso, K3, yf, K7, yf, K3, K2 tog, (K1, yf, K1) into next st, rep from * ending last rep Kfb instead of (K1, yf, K1) into next st.
Row 10 P1, *P5, K9, P6, rep from *.

Row 11 Kfb, *K1, sl 1, K1, psso, K13, K2 tog, K1, (K1, yf, K1) into next st, rep from * ending last rep Kfb instead of (K1, yf, K1) into next st.
Row 12 P1, *P2, P2 tog, P1, K9, P1, P2 tog tbl, P3, rep from *.
Row 13 Kfb, *K2, sl 1, K1, psso, K9, K2 tog, K2, (K1, yf, K1) into next st, rep from * ending last rep Kfb instead of (K1, yf, K1) into next st.
Row 14 P1, *P4, K9, P5, rep from *.
Row 15 Kfb, *K3, sl 1, K1, psso, K7, K2 tog, K3, (K1, yf, K1) into next st, rep from * ending last rep Kfb instead of (K1, yf, K1) into next st.
Row 16 As Row 8.
Row 17 Kfb, *K4, sl 1, K1, psso, K5, K2 tog, K4, (K1, yf, K1) into next st, rep from * ending last rep Kfb instead of (K1, yf, K1) into next st.
Row 18 As Row 6.
Row 19 K1, *yf, K5, sl 1, K1, psso, K3, K2 tog, K5, yf, K1 rep from *.
Row 20 As Row 4.
Row 21 K1, *K1, yf, K5, sl 1, K1, psso, K1, K2 tog, K5, yf, K2, rep from * to end.
Row 22 As Row 2.
Row 23 K1, *K2, yf, K5, sl 1, K2 tog, psso, K5, yf, K3, rep from *.

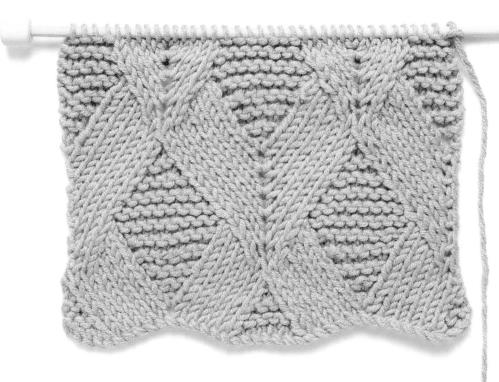

Row 24 K1, *K3, P11, K4, rep from *.

Row 25 K1, *K3, yf, K3, K2 tog, (K1, yf, K1) into next st, sl 1, K1, psso, K3, yf, K4, rep from *.

Row 26 K1, *K4, P11, K5, rep from *.

Row 27 K1, *K6, K2 tog, K1, (K1, yf, K1) into next st, K1, sl 1, K1, psso, K7, rep from *.

Row 28 K1, *K4, P1, P2 tog tbl, P5, P2 tog, P1, K5, rep from *.

Row 29 K1, *K4, K2 tog, K2, (K1, yf, K1) into next st, K2, sl 1, K1, psso, K5, rep from *.

Row 30 K1, *K4, P9, K5, rep from *.

Row 31 K1, *K3, K2 tog, K3, (K1, yf, K1) into next st, K3, sl 1, K1, psso, K4, rep from *.

Row 32 As Row 24.

candle flames

multiple of 12 plus 2 extra

Note In this pattern the number of sts varies from row to row. Accurate count of sts may be made on Row 12 or 24.

Row 1 (RS) *P2, yon, K1, yrn, P2, K2, K2 tog, K3, rep from * to last 2 sts, P2.

Row 2 *K2, P6, K2, P3, rep from * to last 2 sts, K2.

Row 3 *P2, K1, (yf, K1) twice, P2, K2, K2 tog, K2, rep from * to last 2 sts, P2.

Row 4 *(K2, P5) twice, rep from * to last 2 sts, K2.

Row 5 *P2, K2, yf, K1, yf, K2, P2, K2, K2 tog, K1, rep from * to last 2 sts, P2.

Row 6 *K2, P4, K2, P7, rep from * to last 2 sts, K2.

Row 7 *P2, K3, yf, K1, yf, K3, P2, K2, K2 tog, rep from * to last 2 sts, P2.

Row 8 *K2, P3, K2, P9, rep from * to last 2 sts, K2.

Row 9 *P2, K2, K2 tog, K5, P2, K1, K2 tog, rep from * to last 2 sts, P2.

Row 10 *K2, P2, K2, P8, rep from * to last 2 sts, K2.

Row 11 *P2, K2, K2 tog, K4, P2, K2 tog, rep from * to last 2 sts, P2.

Row 12 *K2, P1, K2, P7, rep from * to last 2 sts, K2.

Row 13 *P2, K2, K2 tog, K3, P2, yon, K1, yrn, rep from * to last 2 sts, P2.

Row 14 *K2, P3, K2, P6, rep from * to last 2 sts, K2.

Row 15 *P2, K2, K2 tog, K2, P2, (K1, yf) twice, K1, rep from * to last 2 sts, P2.

Row 16 *(K2, P5) twice, rep from * to last 2 sts, K2.

Row 17 *P2, K2, K2 tog, K1, P2, K2, yf, K1, yf, K2, rep from * to last 2 sts, P2.

Row 18 *K2, P7, K2, P4, rep from * to last 2 sts, K2.

Row 19 *P2, K2, K2 tog, P2, K3, yf, K1, yf, K3, rep from * to last 2 sts, P2.

Row 20 *K2, P9, K2, P3, rep from * to last 2 sts, K2.

Row 21 *P2, K1, K2 tog, P2, K2, K2 tog, K5, rep from * to last 2 sts, P2.

Row 22 *K2, P8, K2, P2, rep from * to last 2 sts, K2.

Row 23 *P2, K2 tog, P2, K2, K2 tog, K4, rep from * to last 2 sts, P2.

Row 24 *K2, P7, K2, P1, rep from * to last 2 sts, K2.

needle sizes

A commercial knitting pattern will specify the size(s) of needles recommended for achieving the stated tension. However, if you are making some experimental tension swatches, perhaps with a view to designing an original garment, you may find the following guidelines helpful. Bear in mind that the recommended size for a given weight of yarn is just a starting point; you may wish to move up or down one or two sizes in order to achieve the best effect with the yarn and stitch pattern you are using.

Yarn	Needle size	Yarn	Needle size
2-ply	2 mm	double knitting	4 mm
3-ply	2¾ mm	Aran	5 mm
4-ply	3 mm	chunky	6 mm
		extra-chunky	9 mm

equivalent needle sizes

This chart shows you how the different knitting needle-size systems compare.

UK	Metric	US	UK	Metric	US
14	2 mm	0	6	5 mm	8
13	2.25 mm	1	5	5.5 mm	9
12	2.75 mm	2	4	6 mm	10
11	3 mm	–	3	6.5 mm	10½
10	3.25 mm	3	2	7 mm	10½
–	3.5 mm	4	1	7.5 mm	11
9	3.75 mm	5	0	8 mm	11
8	4 mm	6	000	9 mm	13
7	4.5 mm	7	0000	10 mm	15

index

acknowledgements

Executive Editor Katy Denny
Project Editor Jessica Cowie
Executive Art Editor Darren Southern
Designer Beverly Price, one2six creative
Copy-editor Kate Haxell
Swatch Knitter Pauline Hornsby
Pattern Checker Sue Horan
Production Manager Ian Paton

The Publishers would like to thank the
following organisations:
John Lewis plc for providing the yarn
for stitch samples – www.johnlewis.com
Susan Cropper at Loop for lending
haberdashery items for photography –
www.loop.gb.com

Picture credits
Octopus Publishing Group Limited/Vanessa
Davies 8-9, 11, 15, 16, 17, 22, 23, 46-47, 51, 65, 70,
96-97, 134-135, 158-159, 167, 196, 202, 204, 216-
217; /Andy Komorowski 1, 2, 5, 24, 25, 29, 30, 32,
33, 34, 35, 36, 37, 38, 39, 40, 41, 42, 43, 44, 45, 54, 55
top, 55 bottom, 74, 76, 77, 78, 79, 80, 81, 82, 84, 85,
86, 87, 88, 89, 90, 91, 92, 93, 94, 95, 98, 111, 112, 114,
115, 116, 117, 118, 119, 120, 122, 123, 124, 125, 126,
128, 129, 130, 131, 132, 133, 137, 150 left, 150 right,
151 left, 151 right, 152, 154, 155, 156, 157, 161 top,
161 bottom, 163 top, 163 bottom, 170, 171, 172, 174,
175, 176, 177, 178, 179, 180, 182, 183, 184, 185, 186,
187, 188, 190, 191, 192, 193, 194, 195, 210, 212, 213,
214, 215, 218, 224, 242, 244, 245, 247, 249, 251;
/Adrian Pope 12, 49; /Gareth Sambidge 107